SIMPLY
CHRISTIANITY

BEYOND RELIGION

JOHN DICKSON

MANY THANKS
Buff for deep love and patience.

·

Josh and Sophie for the delightful interruptions.

·

The people of St. Clement's for the years
of support and critique, and for being a sounding
board for much of this material.

·

Dr. P. T. O'Brien for first teaching me to read Luke.

·

Dominic and Shoonagh for the 'views'.

·

John H. for the valuable suggestions.

·

Deb, Nick, Anna, Sharon, Craig, Therese,
Beck, David, Julie, Alex and Adele—
the 'guinea pigs' in the *Simply Christianity* project.

FOR SOPHIE

Copyright © 1999 Matthias Media
St Matthias Press Ltd ACN 067 558 365

PO Box 225, Kingsford NSW Australia 2032
Telephone: (02) 9663 1478   Facsimile: (02) 9662 4289
International: +61-2-9663 1478   Facsimile: +61-2-9662 4289
Email: info@matthiasmedia.com.au
Website: www.matthiasmedia.com.au

St Matthias Press (UK)
PO Box 665, London SW20 8RU, England
Telephone: (0181) 942 0880   Facsimile: (0181) 942 0990
E-mail: MattMedia@compuserve.com

ISBN 1 876326 18 2

Cover design and typesetting
by Joy Lankshear Design Pty Ltd.

Printed in Australia.

Contents

PART ONE

JESUS
NOW AND
THEN

CHAPTER I

WHICH CHRISTIANITY?

The aeroplane had lost power to all its engines.

As it plummeted towards earth, the pilot announced to the terrified passengers, "I'm sorry, but there are five of us and only four parachutes. I'm the pilot, it's my plane, so I'm taking the first one." He promptly strapped on one of the parachutes and jumped out.

Remaining on the aircraft were a young father, an elite scientist, a minister of religion and a backpacker.

The father stood up and said, "Look, I've got a young family to care for. I've got to take one of the parachutes." He threw it on his back and jumped out.

The scientist immediately insisted, "I am one of the greatest minds in the country and I would be sorely missed. I have to take one of the parachutes." He put it on and jumped out.

The minister turned to the backpacker and began to say, "Listen, my son. I have lived a long and happy life—why don't you…"

But the young man interrupted, "There's no need. That scientist just jumped out with my backpack on".

It is easy to assume that you have the 'real thing' when, in fact, you have only a poor substitute.

In a vaguely Christianised culture like ours it is all too easy to assume that our acceptance or rejection (or perhaps simply avoidance) of the Christian Faith is based on a reasonable knowledge of the topic. I, for one, grew up supposing that the few bits and pieces I'd accidentally picked up at school, through friends and in the media were enough to arrive at the opinion that Christianity was nice for other people. I decided this without once having gone inside a church, or read anything of the Bible, let alone opened a book such as this one.

This book is written in the belief that it is just possible, based on my own experience at least, that the version of Christianity some of us have accepted, rejected or avoided, is not the real thing after all, but an inadequate substitute. The goal of the book, then, is to provide the reader with a clear explanation of real or 'normal' Christianity. You can then decide whether or not the Christian parachute, as it were, is worth strapping onto the back.

One of the common reasons people avoid looking into Christianity in any detail is the simple fact that there are so many Christianities out there to investigate. There's Anglican Christianity, Presbyterian Christianity, Roman Catholic Christianity, Baptist Christianity, and the list goes on. Some of us look at all this and quite reasonably ask, "If the Christians can't make up their mind what they believe, what hope have I got?"

Let me make clear up front that this book does not focus on the teachings of a particular church or denomination but on those facts about Jesus Christ that Christians throughout the last 2000 years have generally agreed upon. It is not necessarily *Anglican* Christianity or *Presbyterian* Christianity or any other sort—it is simply Christianity. This means that the argumentation and hair-splitting that goes on between the major 'brands' of Christianity will be deliberately side-stepped. This is not because these contentions are irrelevant. It's because this book is written for those of us who approach the subject from a distance, who want to look into the ancient Faith with a telescope rather than a magnifying glass.

So, if Christianity minus the myths, rituals and dogma grabs your interest, perhaps this book will answer some of your questions.

At its heart, Christianity is not a beautifully complex philo-sophical system like Buddhism, a towering code of morals like Islam, or a delicate set of rituals as some Christian churches have presented it. The crucial starting point for any discussion about this topic is the fact that 'Christianity'—as the word suggests—is all about a person, Jesus Christ. In fact, Christianity may (and will in this book) be defined simply as, 'Responding appropriately to the news about Jesus Christ'.

This starting point takes the pressure off a little. It means that to grasp Christianity you do not need to wrestle with an entirely new world-view, or adopt a rigorous ethical frame-work, or rehearse a set of foreign ceremonies. Learning about the Christian faith should be more like listening to someone tell a jolly good story or, perhaps more accurately, like tuning in to an important news-flash on the TV.

This may sound odd, particularly if your previous experi-ence of religion came in an ethical, philosophical or ceremonial package, but, as the book unfolds, hopefully it will become clear.

CHAPTER 2

CHRIST IN HISTORY?

Some years ago, just before Christmas day, a TV documentary series on the life of Christ was screened. Far from promoting the 'Christ' part of *Christ*mas, the show claimed to cast 'serious doubts' over the reliability of our knowledge about Jesus of Nazareth. One of the people interviewed on the program, a professor from a large German university, even stated that "Jesus probably never existed at all". The man sounded smart—German accents tend to do that—and he was a professor after all, so I was left with some questions: Is the Christian faith built on an invention or a myth? What and how do we know about Christ? Indeed, did he exist at all?

Only much later did I learn that the sceptical professor in the documentary was actually a professor of modern German literature. He was not a historian at all. He had a fancy title and was no doubt a highly intelligent man, but he was about as 'expert' on the question of the life of Christ as a professor of music would be on the existence of black holes. It turns out that the producers of the TV program had searched long and hard for a historian who would go on camera and deny the reality of Jesus' existence. When they couldn't find one they resorted to an 'expert' from another field, without letting the audience in on the secret. Since then I have discovered that finding a professional historian who denies the first century existence of Jesus Christ is about as difficult as finding a professional scientist who rejects the existence of DNA.

So then, historically speaking, how and what do we really know about the man Jesus Christ? Many, many books have been written on this topic so the following pages are offered only as a summary of some of the relevant points.

Our knowledge of the life of Jesus Christ derives mostly from ancient documents of two types: those written by non-Christians in the period shortly after Christ and those written by Christians. Of course, there are many more Christian texts than non-Christian ones, but this is to be expected, since obviously Christians were highly motivated to preserve the facts about their leader. To offer a modern parallel, I imagine more financial documents have been produced by economists this century than by rock musicians, and certainly more lyrics have been written by pop artists than by financiers!

Nevertheless, the few documents we have from non-Christian sources in the ancient period provide some interesting pieces of information about the life of Jesus. In fact, it may surprise you to know that the broad outline of Christ's life can be known from these references, without even turning to the Christian documents. Let me quote just four of the six references from antiquity.

Flavius Josephus, a Jewish historian writing around 80 AD, mentions Jesus on two separate occasions in his books. In his multi-volume work *The Antiquities of the Jews* (Book 18, chapter three) he writes about Jesus in the following way:

> *Now about this time there lived a wise man called Jesus... Indeed, he was a man who performed startling feats. He was a teacher of the people... and he drew in many from*

*among both the Jews and the Greeks. And those who were
devoted to him from the start did not cease their devotion
even after Governor Pilate, on the basis of charges laid
against him by our leaders, condemned him to a cross.
For [it is reported] he appeared to them alive again… And
the group of 'Christians', named after him, has still not
disappeared to this day.*[†]

A little later in the work (Book 20, chapter nine), Josephus
recounts the execution of one of Jesus' brothers (yes, Jesus had
several younger brothers and sisters), and in so doing, again
makes passing reference to Jesus:

*But this younger Ananus, who, as we have told you
already, took the high priesthood, was a bold man in his
temper, and very insolent… he assembled the Sanhedrin of
judges, and brought before them the brother of Jesus whom*

[†] This passage is the subject of much discussion by historians. Because it does not
appear in some ancient versions of Josephus' book, and because it appears so
favourable toward Jesus, some scholars have conjectured that the passage is a small
piece of 'holy fraud' added into some ancient copies of the *Antiquities* by an over-
zealous Christian copyist. This is overly sceptical, however, and certainly not the
position of the majority of historians. It does appear that a Christian scribe somewhere along the line may have added to Josephus' original comments, trying to
make them more 'glowing' or perhaps more 'doctrinally correct' than they originally appeared. However, a majority of scholars in the field believe that it is possible, on the basis of careful historical and linguistic analysis, to detect what
Josephus was likely to have penned. In the above quotation, I have erred on the
side of caution, removing the probable 'Christian additions' and leaving behind
those statements which historians more expert than I regard as Josephus' original
comments about Jesus. If you're keen to pursue this further and have access to a
major library read, C. A. Evans, *Noncanonical Writings and New Testament Inter-
pretation* (Massachusetts: Hendrickson Publishers, 1992) pages 86-96. Or if you
are a total glutton for punishment read, G. H. Twelftree, "Jesus in Jewish Traditions", in *Gospel Perspectives: Studies of History and Tradition in the Four Gospels*
(Vol. 5) (Manchester: JSOT Press, 1981) pages 289-341.

they call the Christ, whose name was James, and some others, and when he had formed an accusation against them as breakers of the law, he delivered them to be stoned to death...

This text is fascinating for historians of early Christianity. The New Testament (the second half of the Bible) recounts a little about Jesus' brother, James. We know, for instance, that although he started out a sceptic about his famous brother's career, he ended up being one of the key early Christian leaders, claiming even to be an eyewitness to Jesus' resurrection. Our biblical information about James, however, cuts off with him still alive and well in Jerusalem, actively proclaiming the significance of Jesus. What Josephus writes completes the picture. Obviously, James' efforts to promote the message about his brother ran foul of the authorities and, just like his brother 25 years before, James found himself paying the supreme price of his own life.

Cornelius Tacitus is regarded as ancient Rome's greatest historian. His *Annals of Imperial Rome*, written shortly after Josephus (in 115 AD), are the basis of much of our most accurate information about Emperors Tiberius, Claudius, Nero, and many of the other famous figures of the period. In recounting the persecutions against the early Christians, Tacitus records the following about Jesus:

Christians derived their name from a man called Christ, who, during the reign of Emperor Tiberius had been executed by sentence of the procurator Pontius Pilate. The deadly superstition, thus checked for the moment, broke out afresh not only in Judaea, the first source of the evil, but also in the City of Rome, where all things hideous and shameful from every part of the world meet and become popular.

Cornelius Tacitus, Annals of Imperial Rome *(25.44)*

As you can tell from his comments, Tacitus was not exactly a 'fan' of Christ or of the early Christians. Yet as a matter of historical accuracy Tacitus feels it necessary to include a reference to Jesus and confirm some details about his execution—where, when and by whom. Though Tacitus provides no new information about Christ, it does confirm from the Roman side some of the details we already knew. It also shows that the events of Jesus' life had a significant enough impact around the Mediterranean to gain the attention (and disdain) of an elite Roman intellectual on the other side of the Empire. That a wandering Jewish peasant-teacher from Palestine rated a mention at all in Tacitus' *Annals of Imperial Rome* is surprising.

Lastly, another small piece of information deriving from the second century comes from a Jewish religious document called the **Talmud.** Although Jesus himself had been a popular Jewish teacher a century or so before, as time passed a number of very unflattering opinions were being formed about him:

> *Jesus of Nazareth was hung up on the day of preparation for the Passover… because he practiced sorcery and he led Israel astray.*
>
> *Baraitha Sanhedrin 43a*

It is difficult to know exactly what to make of this statement, since it is clearly a piece of official anti-Christian propaganda from a century or more after Jesus. Nevertheless, it does confirm that Jewish people of the second century thought Jesus to have been a real figure who had had a dramatic effect on many of their Palestinian Jewish forebears ('he lead Israel astray'). It also provides historians with another piece of corroborating evidence to support the wide-ranging claim that Jesus had performed unusual (miraculous?) feats. For it is curious that the statement makes no attempt to deny the rumoured exploits of Jesus. Instead, conceding that Jesus had inexplicable abilities, the document tries to explain them away as 'sorcery', something Jewish people were forbidden to be involved with.

If we piece together all the information contained in the above references it is fascinating that just about the whole story of Jesus can be uncovered, without even opening a Bible. We learn:

- when he lived
- where he lived
- that he was an influential teacher
- that he engaged in activities thought to be supernatural
- that he was executed; when and by whom
- that he had a brother called James who was also executed
- that people claimed to have seen him raised from the dead
- that he was widely known by the prestigious title 'the Christ'

This is a lot of material to glean from documents composed by people who were anything but supporters of the Christian faith.

None of these texts actually 'proves' Christianity. Statements made by non-Christians are no more trustworthy than those by Christians. From the historian's point of view, we must look at non-Christian accounts with the same healthy suspicion we apply to biblical documents. Nevertheless, the interesting thing is that whatever the sources, biases and (mis)information lying behind each of these documents, taken as a whole, they substantially corroborate the picture of

Jesus presented in the earliest Christian literature. This is rather good news for anyone interested in enquiring into the Bible's version of the events surrounding Jesus' life. Indeed, one of Australia's most eminent ancient historians, Emeritus Professor E. A. Judge of Macquarie University, Sydney, has recently commented:

> *An ancient historian has no problem seeing the phenomenon of Jesus as an historical one. His many surprising aspects only help anchor him in history. Myth or legend would have created a more predictable figure. The writings that sprang up about Jesus also reveal to us a movement of thought and an experience of life so unusual that something much more substantial than the imagination is needed to explain it. (Quoted in P. Barnett, The Truth about Jesus, Aquila, Sydney, 1994)*

CHRIST IN BIOGRAPHY

Although the non-Christian references to Jesus provide a historical 'grounding' for the life of Jesus, they do not provide us with the detail we need to assess the importance of Jesus for our lives. So, for instance, although they tell us *that* he taught, they say nothing about *what* he taught; again, although they inform us *that* he died, they reveal nothing of the significance Jesus himself placed on his death, and so on. To know these things we need to turn to some other, even more ancient, documents.

Our detailed knowledge of Christ comes from the biographies of his life written in the middle to late first century AD. Since Jesus died around 33AD, this is a time gap of only 30-60 years after the events. This makes these documents among the most chronologically proximate historical texts from the ancient world (that is, written close in time to the events they describe). Tacitus, for instance, wrote about events that had occurred over a century earlier, and yet his writings are still rightly regarded by all scholars as superb historical sources.

These biographies of Jesus are called 'Gospels' (meaning literally 'grand-news') and there are four of them. Originally, they circulated somewhat independently of each other, but within about 50 years or so they were brought together, along with a collection of letters written by early Christian leaders, to form what would eventually be called the New Testament, that is, the second section of the Bible.

The four biographies, or Gospels, are titled after the name of their probable author. They each have their own particular 'angle' on Jesus:

THE GOSPEL OF MATTHEW is famous for its lengthy record of Jesus' great ethical teachings. Many of those great sayings you may have heard—'turn the other cheek'; 'blessed are the peacemakers'; 'our Father who art in Heaven'—come from Matthew's biography.

THE GOSPEL OF MARK is famous for its short, punchy style. It is a brilliant read if you've only got about an hour to discover the meaning of the world's most influential man.

THE GOSPEL OF LUKE is famous for its emphasis on Jesus' friendship with 'non-religious' people. Here we read about Jesus criticising the hypocritical religious hierarchy of his day and yet welcoming prostitutes, criminals and greedy businessmen.

THE GOSPEL OF JOHN is famous for its profound insight into the nature of Jesus. Although the story is the same, the angle at which John comes at Jesus is quite amazing.

Simply Christianity is based entirely on the Gospel of Luke. I chose this biography partly because of its focus on Jesus' friendships with the 'not-so-religious'. This makes it the ideal read for anyone who feels religious matters are a little foreign, or for whom Christianity is little more than a distant 'Sunday-School' memory. Although it is not as short as Mark's biography, there are still less words in Luke than in the sports section in Monday's paper or the gig guide in Thursday's paper. For a book written almost 2000 years ago on the other side of the world, it's actually a very easy read.

Luke, a medical doctor and historian, probably composed his biography some time between 70-80AD, though his research for the book no doubt began at a much earlier date. He had not personally known Christ, but the evidence suggests that he had spoken with, and based his work on, those who had. Several times during the 50's AD, Luke even had the privileged experience of travelling and working with one of the key eyewitnesses to Jesus' resurrection, a man known as the Apostle Paul, who wrote many of the other books of the New Testament. For Luke, this must have been a time of great inspiration as well as fruitful research for his own account of the life of Jesus. These experiences, combined with the fact that he was a man of high education (as indicated by the fine literary Greek of his biography) made him perfectly suited to produce a work of such historical importance.

A major part of my book is designed to help you read Luke's book. There is nothing like reading a primary source for yourself. This way, rather than simply relying on a modern writer like me telling you what Christianity is all about, you'll be able to test my explanations, experiences and analogies by comparing them to the original biography itself.

To make it easier, I've included a modern English translation of Luke's biography within the pages of this book. It appears in four parts. Before each part I'll provide a brief introduction, indicating some of the big ideas to look out for as you read it. Then you'll be in Luke's hands as he recounts the events from that period of Jesus' life. Then, after you've read that part of Luke, it'll be back to me. I'll spend a few chapters unpacking Luke's material and drawing out some implications for our lives now. Then I'll introduce the next section of Luke, and so on. Slowly but surely I hope that what will emerge from these pages—particularly those containing Luke's words—is a picture of Christianity that strips away the myths, rituals and dogma often associated with 'religion' and leaves us with the man himself, Jesus of Nazareth.

So then, at the very least, by the end of the book you'll be able to say that you've read one whole book of the Bible and know exactly what it says about Christ. You'll be able to boast to your friends that you (probably unlike them) know precisely what Christianity is about and what it is supposed to mean for modern life. That can't be a bad thing.

Of course, focusing on one of the books in the Bible, *Luke*, raises a question for some people: Can we trust what we read there? It is occasionally said that the Gospels (and the Bible generally) are full of 'myths'. Actually, the longer I think and more I read about this issue the more convinced I am that the real myths are those *about* the Gospels, not *in* them. If the reliability of Luke's biography is a concern for you, I've included some material on the topic that you may want to read before you move on to the next section of the book. It can be found at page 201 in the 'Extra Information' section at the back of the book.

In the end, however, the best way to weigh the issues relating to the trustworthiness of the original biographies is to read the books themselves—in our case, to read Luke's biography. With this in mind, the most appropriate way to conclude the first part of this book is probably to quote the opening paragraph of the Gospel of Luke, for here we can see for ourselves Luke's great concern for telling the truth in an ordered fashion.

Like other books from the ancient world, Luke addresses his work to an individual, a man named Theophilus. He was perhaps the financial benefactor in Luke's vast historical project, or perhaps simply an important official interested in a thorough account of the reports about the man Jesus. Whoever he was, Luke was keen to assure him that the account which follows is one worthy of our interest and trust:

> *Since many have attempted to put together an account of the things that have been fulfilled among us (just as these things were passed on to us by those who from the beginning were eyewitnesses and guardians of the message), so it seemed good to me as well, having checked everything very carefully from the start, to write something orderly for you, your excellency, Theophilus. My aim is that you may know the reliability of the reports you have heard.*

Part of the aim of my book too is that you, like old Theophilus, "may know the reliability of the message" about Christ, and discover its relevance for your own life today.

PART TWO

IN THE
PRESENCE
OF
GREATNESS

In the USA some time ago, three lads hopped onto their local bus for a ride. They were in a fairly 'vigorous' mood, so when they noticed a man alone up the back of the bus dressed rather casually in a track-suit and beanie, they thought they'd see how far they could push him.

At first they just made a few light jokes about him. The stranger didn't respond. They turned up the heat and started to insult him directly. The stranger still didn't respond. They continued this for some time trying to get the man to fight back. After all, there were three of them and just one of him.

Eventually the bus arrived at the stranger's stop. He stood up. The lads then realised that he was much, much bigger than they had estimated. He looked down at the young men, reached into his pocket, and pulled out his business card. He handed it to one of them and then silently walked off the bus and on his way.

The three boys huddled around the card to see who this stranger was and what he did for a living. The card read:

Joe Louis
Professional Boxer

For those who don't know their boxing history, these lads had tried to start a fight with the man who would become the heavyweight boxing champion of the world eleven times running. They had been in the presence of greatness and did not know it. Upon reading the business card I assume they instantly felt very small, greatly embarrassed, and extremely grateful that Mr Louis had woken up in a good mood that day.

So what's this got to do with Christianity? In this section we'll begin to read Luke's biography of Jesus. From the word 'go', Luke is at pains to inform his readers that as we look at the life of Christ we are all in the presence of greatness. In fact, these opening chapters of Luke's biography function as a kind of lengthy business card, or C.V., for Jesus Christ. Luke offers it to us in the hope that we, like him, will be impressed with the immense status of this man.

Luke begins with the strange events surrounding Christ's birth, some of which you may recognize from our modern Christmas traditions, but he quickly moves us forward to the first eighteen months of Jesus' three-year public career as an adult. During this whirlwind year and a half of lectures, debates, parties (yes!) and incredible public demonstrations on the part of Jesus, those closest to him—usually called 'disciples'—are led irresistibly to one conclusion: this is no ordinary religious teacher.

As you read, look out for the hints about Jesus' status and identity.

Luke's Biography
Chapters 1–9

CHAPTER 1[†]

Dedication: to Theophilus[††]

Since many have attempted to put together an account of the things that have been fulfilled among us (just as these things were passed on to us by those who from the beginning were eye-witnesses and guardians of the message), so it seemed good to me as well, having checked everything very carefully from the start, to write something orderly for you, Your Excellency, Theophilus. My aim is that you may know the reliability of the reports you have heard.

The Births of John and Jesus

In the time of Herod, King of Judea, there was a certain priest called Zechariah from the priestly division of Abijah. He had a wife, Elizabeth, who was descended from the line of Aaron. They were both righteous people before God, living blamelessly according to all the commands and righteous ways of the Lord. Yet they had no children, because Elizabeth was barren; and they were both well advanced in age.

Now it happened that Zechariah's division was rostered to perform the priestly duties before God, and according to the custom of the priesthood, he was allotted the task of going into the temple of the Lord to burn incense. A large crowd outside the temple was praying at the time the incense was burned.

[†]   The chapter divisions and subheadings are not part of the original Greek text of Luke. They have been added for ease of reading and reference.

[††] Many ancient pieces of literature were dedicated to important individuals, often the sponsor of the work.

An angelic Messenger[†] of the Lord appeared to him, standing at the right of the incense altar, and when he saw this, Zechariah was very troubled and afraid.

The Messenger said to him, "Do not be afraid, Zechariah, because your prayers have been heard—your wife Elizabeth will bear you a son, and you are to give him the name John. He will be a joy and a delight to you, and many will rejoice because of his birth, for he will be great before the Lord. He will not drink wine or strong drink, and he will be filled with the Holy Spirit even from his mother's womb. He will turn many of the sons of Israel back to the Lord their God, and he will go before the Lord in the spirit and power of Elijah, to turn the hearts of fathers to their children, and to turn the disobedient to the wise way of the righteous. He will prepare a people who are ready for the Lord."

Zechariah said to the Messenger, "How will I know this is true? For I am an old man and my wife is advanced in age."

The Messenger replied, "I am Gabriel who stands in the presence of God. I was sent to speak to you, and make this important announcement to you. But now you will be silent and not able to speak until the day these things come about, because you did not believe my message, which will be fulfilled in due course."

While all this was happening, the people were waiting for Zechariah, and wondered why he was taking so long in the temple. When he came out, he was completely unable to speak to them, and they realised that he had seen a vision in the temple. He was making signs to them, and remained speechless.

Eventually, the time of Zechariah's service came to an end, and he went home. After this, Elizabeth his wife became pregnant. She hid herself for five months, and her comment was, "So

† Traditionally, *angel*; also below.

this is how the Lord has acted for me, when he looked kindly on me, and took away my disgrace among the people".

In the sixth month, the angel Gabriel was sent from God to a city in Galilee called Nazareth, to a virgin who was engaged to a man named Joseph. Joseph was from the family line of David, and the virgin's name was Mary. The angelic Messenger went to her and said, "Rejoice, O highly favoured one, the Lord is with you".

But when she heard this, Mary was deeply disturbed, and wondered what sort of greeting this could be.

The Messenger said to her, "Do not be afraid, Mary, for you have found favour with God. You will become pregnant, and bear a son, and you are to call him Jesus. He will be a great one, and will be called 'Son of the Most High', and the Lord God will give him the throne of his father David; and he will rule over the house of Jacob forever, and his kingdom will never end."

Mary said to the Messenger, "How can this be, since I am a virgin?"

The Messenger replied, "The Holy Spirit will come upon you, and the power of the Most High will overshadow you. Therefore the child to be born will be holy, and will be called the Son of God. Look, your cousin Elizabeth has even conceived a son in her old age, and this is the sixth month—she who was supposedly barren. So nothing is impossible for God."

Mary said, "I am the Lord's servant. May it all happen to me just as you say."

And the Messenger left her.

Soon after, Mary got ready and went with some haste to the hill country, to a city in Judah. She entered Zechariah's home, and called out a greeting to Elizabeth.

When Elizabeth heard Mary's greeting, the baby kicked in her womb, and Elizabeth was filled with the Holy Spirit. And she declared in a loud voice, "You are the most blessed of women, and blessed is the fruit of your womb! And who am I that the mother of my Lord should visit me? For as the sound of your greeting reached my ears, the baby within my womb kicked with joy. Blessed is she who believed that what the Lord said to her would take place."

And Mary said:

"My soul greatly honours the Lord,

And my spirit rejoices because of God my Saviour,

for he has taken notice of the humble state of his servant.

For from now on, every generation will call me blessed

because the Mighty One has done great things for me—

His name is holy,

And to generation after generation of people, he shows mercy to those who fear him.

He has shown the strength of his arm, and scattered those who are arrogant in their hearts;

he has knocked down rulers from their thrones; and he has lifted up the humble.

He has filled the hungry with good things; but the rich he has sent away empty-handed.

He has taken care of Israel, his son, remembering to be merciful,

just as he promised to our fathers, to Abraham and his descendants for ever."

Mary remained with her for about three months, and then returned home.

Now the time finally came for Elizabeth to have her baby, and she gave birth to a son. Her neighbours and relatives heard that the Lord had shown her such mercy, and they rejoiced with her.

On the eighth day, they came to have the boy circumcised, and they were going to name him after his father, Zechariah. But his mother said, "No, he is to be called John".

They said to her, "No-one from your family has that name". And they communicated with his father by signs, to see what he wanted to call him.

Zechariah asked for something to write on, and wrote, "His name is John". And they were all amazed.

Immediately, Zechariah's mouth was opened, and his tongue set free, and he began to praise God.

And those who lived nearby were filled with awe, and in the mountain region of Judea there was much discussion about all these events. Everyone who heard about it could not help wondering, "What then will this child turn out to be?" For the hand of the Lord was with him.

And his father Zechariah was filled with the Holy Spirit and prophesied:

"Blessed be the Lord God of Israel, because he has come to us, and redeemed his people;

he has raised up a mighty Saviour[†] for us in the family line of his servant, David,

just as he promised through his holy prophets of old—

rescue[††] from our enemies and from the hand of all who hate us, to show mercy to our fathers and to remember his holy covenant,

an oath which he swore to our father Abraham—to grant us deliverance from the hand of our enemies, and to serve him without fear

in holiness and righteousness in his presence all our days.

And you, my son, will be called a prophet of the Most High; for you will prophesy in advance of the Lord, to prepare his way,

---

† Or *Rescuer*, also below.
†† Or *salvation*.

to make rescue known to his people by the forgiveness of
their sins,
through the compassionate mercy of our God, which will
break on us like a sunrise from on high,
to give light to those who sit in darkness and the shadow
of death,
in order to guide our feet into the way of peace."

The boy grew and became strong in spirit; and he lived in the
desert until the time when he appeared publicly to Israel.

CHAPTER 2

Around that time, a decree went out from Caesar Augustus to con-
duct a census of the known world—this was the first census that
took place when Quirinius was governor of Syria. So everyone travelled back to their home towns to register, including Joseph. He
went up from Nazareth in Galilee to the city of David (which is
called Bethlehem) in Judea, because he was from David's family
line. He took Mary with him to be registered, and she was pregnant.

As it happened, while they were there in Bethlehem, the time
came for her to have the baby, and she gave birth to her firstborn
son. And because there was no room for them in the inn, she used
strips of cloth to wrap him up, and a food trough for his cradle.

In that part of the country, there were shepherds who stayed
out in the fields at night to keep watch over their flock. Without
warning, one of the Lord's angelic Messengers appeared to them,
and the brilliance† of the Lord shone all around them. They were
terrified, but the Messenger said to them, "Do not be afraid. Listen,
I am here to bring you news of great joy which is for all the people:

† Or *glory.*

today, a Saviour has been born to you in the city of David. He is the Lord Christ. And this will be the sign for you—you will find a child wrapped up in strips of cloth and lying in a food trough."

Suddenly, there appeared with the Messenger a vast company of the heavenly armies, praising God and saying, "Glory to God in the highest, and peace on earth to those with whom he is pleased".

After the angels had left them and gone back to heaven, the shepherds said to one another, "Come on, let's go into Bethlehem and see this thing which has taken place, which the Lord has made known to us". They went quickly, and discovered Mary and Joseph—and the baby lying in a food trough.[†] When they saw this, they revealed the message that had been told to them about this child, and everyone who heard it was amazed at what the shepherds said. Mary was taking note of these things, pondering them in her heart. The shepherds went back, glorifying and praising God for everything they had heard and seen, which had happened just as they had been told.

Jesus' Childhood

After eight days, the time came for him to be circumcised, and he was called Jesus, which was what the Messenger said to call him before he was conceived in the womb. And when the days of their purification were over (according to the law of Moses), Joseph and Mary took him up to Jerusalem to present him to the Lord, just as it is written in the Law of the Lord, 'Every firstborn male shall be holy to the Lord'. They also went in order to offer a sacrifice, as the Law of the Lord says: a pair of turtledoves or two young pigeons.

Now there was a man in Jerusalem named Simeon. He was a righteous and devout man, who was waiting for Israel to be

---

† Traditionally, *manger.*

comforted; and the Holy Spirit was upon him. It had been revealed to him by the Holy Spirit that he would not see death before he had seen the Lord's Christ.

Through the influence of the Spirit, he went into the temple. And when the parents of the boy Jesus came in, to do what the custom of the law required concerning him, Simeon took him in his arms and blessed God, and said,

"Now, Master, you may let your servant depart in peace, as you promised,

because with my own eyes I have seen your salvation[†]

which you have prepared for all peoples to see—

a revealing light for the other nations, and so your people Israel will be glorified."

His father and mother were amazed at what was said about him, and Simeon blessed them and said to Mary, his mother, "This one is destined to cause the falling and rising of many in Israel, and to be a sign that is spoken against—and as for you, a sword will pierce your own soul—and thus the thoughts of many hearts will be revealed."

In the temple there was also a prophetess called Anna, the daughter of Phanuel, from the tribe of Asher. She was very old, having lived with her husband seven years after her marriage, and then as a widow for eighty-four years. She never left the temple, worshipping God with fasting and prayers night and day. She came up to them at that very moment, and gave thanks to God, and began to speak about the child to all those who were waiting for the redemption of Jerusalem.

When they had finished all that the Law of the Lord required, Joseph and Mary returned to their own city of Nazareth in Galilee. The boy grew and became strong, and full

† Or *rescue.*

of wisdom. And the grace of God was with him.

Each year his parents went to Jerusalem for the Feast of the Passover[†], and when he was twelve they went up for the Feast according to the custom.

When the days of the Feast were completed, they began their return journey, but the boy Jesus remained behind in Jerusalem without his parents knowing. They thought that he was somewhere in their group, and they had gone a day's journey before they started to look for him among their relatives and friends. Finding nothing, they returned to Jerusalem to search for him. After three days, they found him in the temple, sitting among the teachers, listening to them and asking questions. All those who heard him were astonished at his level of understanding, and his answers.

When they saw him there, his parents were very surprised and his mother said to him, "Son, why did you treat us like this? Look, your father and I have been very worried searching for you."

He said to them, "Why did you have to search for me? Didn't you realise that I must be in my father's house?" But they didn't understand what he was saying to them.

So Jesus went back with his parents to Nazareth, and was obedient to them. And his mother treasured all these things in her heart. Jesus grew in wisdom and stature, and in the favour of God and those who knew him.

CHAPTER 3

Preparations for Jesus' Public Career

It was the fifteenth year of the reign of Tiberius Caesar. Pontius Pilate was governor of Judea, Herod was tetrarch of Galilee, his

† An annual festival celebrating the Exodus of the Israelites from Egypt.

brother Phillip tetrarch of Iturea and Traconitis, and Lysanias was tetrarch of Abilene. It was at this time, during the high priesthood of Annas and Caiaphas, that the word of God came to John, the son of Zechariah, in the desert.

He went throughout the country around the Jordan, proclaiming a baptism[†] of repentance[††] for the forgiveness of sins. As it is written in the scroll of the words of Isaiah the prophet:

"A voice crying out in the desert:

'Prepare the way of the Lord;

make his paths straight;

every valley will be filled in,

and every mountain and hill will be levelled;

the crooked roads will become straight,

and the rough tracks smooth.

And all humanity will see the salvation[*] of God.'"

So John said to the crowds that had come out to be baptized by him, "You snakes! Who warned you to flee from the coming Anger[**]? Therefore, produce fruits that are worthy of repentance. And do not start to say to yourselves, 'We have Abraham as our father'. For I tell you that God is able to raise up children of Abraham from these rocks. Indeed, the axe is already poised at the root of the trees; and every tree that does not produce good fruit is cut down and thrown into the fire."

"What should we do then?" the crowds asked him.

He answered them, "The one who has two shirts should donate one to someone who has none; and the one who has food should do the same".

[†]   An initiation rite common among Jews of the period.
[††] Literally, 'a change of outlook or mind', used here of returning to God.
[*]   i.e. *rescue.*
[**] Or *wrath.*

Tax collectors[†] also came to be baptized by him, and said to him, "Teacher, what should we do?"

And John answered them, "Take no more than you are supposed to collect".

Soldiers also asked him, "What about us; what should we do?"

And he said to them, "Don't threaten people for money, or be corrupt, but be content with your wages".

The expectations of the people began to rise, and everyone wondered in their hearts whether he might not be the Christ.

In answer to this, John said to all of them, "I baptize you with water; but someone much stronger than me is coming—I would not even be worthy to undo the strap of his sandal. He will baptize you with the Holy Spirit and fire. He has the winnowing fork in his hand to clean out his threshing floor, and gather the grain into his barn. But he will burn up the chaff with unquenchable fire."

Thus, with many other warnings, John announced the news to the people.

But when John rebuked Herod the tetrarch for taking Herodias, his brother's wife, and for all the other wicked things he had done, Herod added this to them all: he locked up John in prison.

Now when all the people had been baptized, and Jesus also had been baptized and was praying, heaven was opened, and the Holy Spirit came down upon him in the form of a dove. And a voice came from heaven, "You are my beloved son; with you I am very pleased."

....

† That is, Jews who collaborated with the occupying Roman forces to collect taxes from their fellow Jews. They were widely hated, and excluded from Jewish religious life.

Jesus himself was about thirty when it all really began. He was the son (so it was thought) of Joseph:

who was the son of Heli,
the son of Matthat,
the son of Levi,
the son of Melchi,
the son of Jannai,
the son of Joseph,
the son of Mattathias,
the son of Amos,
the son of Nahum,
the son of Esli,
the son of Naggai,
the son of Maath,
the son of Mattathias,
the son of Semein,
the son of Josech,
the son of Joda,
the son of Jo-anan,
the son of Rhesa,
the son of Zerubbabel,
the son of Shealtiel,
the son of Neri,
the son of Melchi,
the son of Addi,
the son of Cosam,
the son of Elmadam,
the son of Er,
the son of Joshua,
the son of Eliezer,
the son of Jorim,
the son of Matthat,

the son of Levi,
the son of Simeon,
the son of Judah,
the son of Joseph,
the son of Jonam,
the son of Eliakim,
the son of Melea,
the son of Menna,
the son of Mattatha,
the son of Nathan,
the son of David,
the son of Jesse,
the son of Obed,
the son of Boaz,
the son of Sala,
the son of Nahshon,
the son of Amminadab,
the son of Admin,
the son of Arni,
the son of Hezron,
the son of Perez,
the son of Judah,
the son of Jacob,
the son of Isaac,
the son of Abraham,
the son of Terah,
the son of Nahor,
the son of Serug,
the son of Reu,
the son of Peleg,

the son of Eber,
the son of Shelah,
the son of Cainan,
the son of Arphaxad,
the son of Shem,
the son of Noah,
the son of Lamech,
the son of Methuselah,

the son of Enoch,
the son of Jared,
the son of Mahalaleel,
the son of Cainan,
the son of Enosh,
the son of Seth,
the son of Adam,
the son of God.

CHAPTER 4

Full of the Holy Spirit, Jesus returned from the Jordan and was brought by the Spirit into the desert for forty days, where he was tested by the devil.

During that time he ate nothing, and by the end of it he was hungry. So the devil said to him, "If you are the son of God, tell this rock to become bread".

But Jesus answered him, "It is written in the Scriptures, 'Man will not live by bread alone'".

Then the devil led him up high and showed him all the kingdoms of the world in a moment of time. And the devil said to him, "I will give all this authority to you, and the glory of all these kingdoms, because it is mine to give. And I can give it to anyone I wish. If, then, you will worship me, all of it will be yours."

But Jesus replied, "It is written, 'You are to worship the Lord your God, and serve him alone'".

Then he took him to Jerusalem, stood him on the pinnacle of the temple and said to him, "If you are the son of God, throw yourself down from here, for it is written, 'He will commands his angels concerning you, to keep watch over you', and 'They will bear you up on their hands, in case you should strike your foot against a rock'".

Jesus answered him, "It is said, 'Do not put the Lord your

God to the test'".

And when the devil had finished every test, he left Jesus until an opportune time.

Jesus Begins his Public Career in Galilee[†]

Jesus returned in the power of the Spirit to Galilee, and a report about him spread throughout the whole region. He taught in their synagogues, and everybody spoke glowingly of him.

He came to Nazareth where he had grown up, and according to his custom, he went into the synagogue on the Sabbath[††] day. He stood up to read, and the scroll of the prophet Isaiah was handed to him. Unrolling it, he found the place where it was written,

"The Spirit of the Lord is upon me, because he has anointed me to announce great news to the poor; he has sent me to proclaim release for prisoners, and sight once more for the blind, to send the oppressed away free; to proclaim the acceptable year of the Lord".

Rolling up the scroll, he gave it to the assistant and sat down. And the eyes of everyone in the synagogue were fixed on him.

He began to speak to them, "Today, this Scripture is fulfilled in your hearing".

And they were all speaking about him, and were amazed at the gracious words which came out of his mouth. They said, "Isn't this Joseph's son?"

And he said to them, "No doubt you will quote this proverb to me, 'Physician, heal yourself! What we have heard you did in Capernaum, do here as well in your home town.'"

But he went on, "Truly, I tell you that no prophet is acceptable in his home town. Truly, I tell you, there were many widows

[†] That is, the northern part of Israel.
[††] That is, from Friday night to Saturday night, the day of rest set down in the Law of Moses.

in Elijah's time in Israel, when the heavens were shut for three years and six months, and a great famine settled on the whole land. Elijah was sent to none of them, but to the widow of Zarephath in Sidon. And there were many lepers in Israel in the time of Elisha the prophet, but none of them were cleansed; only Naaman the Syrian."

When they heard this in the synagogue, they were all filled with rage. Rising up, they ran him out of the city, and led him to the edge of the cliff on which their city was built, in order to throw him down. But he passed straight through their midst, and went on his way.

Then he went down to Capernaum, which was a city in Galilee, and he was teaching them on the Sabbath Day. They were astonished at his teaching, because he spoke with authority.

Now in the synagogue there was a man with an unclean demonic spirit, and he called out in a loud voice, "Hey! What have you to do with us, Jesus of Nazareth? Have you come to destroy us? I know who you are: the holy one of God!"

Jesus rebuked him, and said, "Be silent, and come out of him". And after hurling the man down in their midst, the demon came out of him. The man was unharmed.

They were all awe-struck, and said to one another, "What sort of word is this, that commands the unclean spirits with authority and power, and they come out?"

And reports about him spread throughout the region.

Jesus stood up and left the synagogue, and went to Simon's house. Simon's mother-in-law was in the grip of a high fever, and they asked him to do something for her.

Jesus stood over her and rebuked the fever, and it left her. She got straight up and began to serve them.

As the sun was setting, everyone who had any who were sick

with various diseases brought them to him. He laid his hands on each one of them, and healed them. And demons were coming out of many people, calling out, "You are the son of God!" Yet Jesus rebuked them, and would not allow them to speak, because they knew that he was the Christ.

When it was day, he went out into a place in the desert, and the crowds were looking for him. But he said to them, "I must announce the good news of the kingdom of God to the other cities as well, because that is why I was sent."

And he went on preaching in the synagogues of Galilee.

CHAPTER 5

On one occasion, he was standing by Lake Gennesaret and the crowd was pressing in on him to hear the message of God. He saw two boats on the edge of the lake, left there by the fishermen who were cleaning the nets. He got into one of the boats, which belonged to Simon, and asked him to put out a little way from the land. When he had sat down, he taught the crowd from the boat.

When he had finished speaking, he said to Simon, "Put out into the deeper water, and let down your nets for a catch".

Simon answered, "Master, we have been working hard all night without getting a thing. But if you say so, I will let down the nets."

Having done so, they netted a huge quantity of fish, and their nets began to tear. They waved to their partners in the other boat to come and help them, and they came and filled both boats to the point of sinking.

Seeing all this, Simon Peter[†] fell at Jesus' knees and said, "Go

† Jesus later gave Simon the additional name 'Peter'.

away from me, Lord, for I am a sinful man". For he was gripped with fear and amazement (as were all those with him) at the catch of fish they had taken. James and John, the sons of Zebedee, who were Simon's partners, felt the same. And Jesus said to Simon, "Don't be afraid. From now on, you will catch people."

And after they had brought the boats to shore, they left everything, and followed him.

In one of the cities Jesus was visiting, there was a man covered with leprosy. When he saw Jesus, he fell down before him and begged him, "Lord, if you are willing, you can make me clean".

Jesus stretched out his hand and touched him, and said, "I am willing. Be clean." And immediately the leprosy disappeared. Jesus commanded the man not to say anything. "Instead, go and show yourself to the priest, and bring the offerings for your purification, as Moses commanded. This will be a testimony to them."

But reports about him spread all the more, and a great crowd gathered to hear him and to be healed from their sicknesses.

But he used to withdraw into the desert and pray.

One day, Jesus was teaching, and some Pharisees† and teachers of the Law†† were sitting there. They had come from all the towns of Galilee and Judea and Jerusalem. And the power of the Lord was with him to heal.

Some men arrived carrying a paralysed man on a stretcher. They were trying to bring him in to put him before Jesus, but because of the crowd, they could find no way through. They went up onto the roof of the house, and lowered him down on his stretcher through the tiles, right into their midst in front of Jesus. When Jesus saw their faith, he said, "Friend, your sins are forgiven".

The Scribes and Pharisees began to think to themselves,

† A strict religious group among the Jews.
†† Also described in Luke as 'Scribes' and 'religious lawyers'.

"Who is this who speaks such blasphemies? Who is able to forgive sins except God alone?"

But Jesus realised what they were thinking, and answered them, "Why do you think this way in your hearts? Which is easier: to say, 'Your sins are forgiven' or to say, 'Get up and walk'? But so that you may know that the Son of Man[†] has authority on earth to forgive sins…" He said to the paralysed man, "I tell you, get up, and pick up your stretcher and go back home".

And immediately he got up right there in front of them, picked up what he was lying on and went back to his home, giving honour and praise to God.

Everybody was stunned, and honoured God. They were quite afraid, and said, "We have seen extraordinary things today".

After this, Jesus went out and saw a tax collector named Levi sitting at the tax collecting booth. He said to him, "Follow me", and he got up, left everything, and followed him. And Levi held a great feast for Jesus at his house, with a large crowd of tax collectors; and others were there as well, reclining at the table with them[††].

Now the Pharisees and Scribes complained to his disciples, "Why do you eat and drink with tax collectors and sinners?"

And Jesus replied, "It is not the healthy who need a doctor, but the sick. I have not come to invite the righteous, but sinners to repentance."

They said to him, "John's disciples are always fasting and praying, and so are the disciples of the Pharisees. But yours eat and drink!"

....

[†] 'Son of Man' was a common Jewish way of referring to oneself in the third person (as 'oneself' is in English). Jesus also used this expression to refer back to an exalted figure in Old Testament prophecy, the 'Son of Man' of Daniel 7.
[††] People did not sit on chairs to eat in the ancient world; they had low tables, and reclined on cushions or couches to eat.

Jesus replied, "Are you able to make wedding guests fast while the bridegroom is with them? But the days will come when the bridegroom is taken away from them, and then they will fast."

He also told them this parable[†]: "No-one tears a piece off a new garment and sews it onto an old one—you would not only ruin the new one, but the piece from the new would not match the old. And no-one pours young wine into old wineskins—the young wine would burst the wineskins, the wine would spill everywhere, and the wineskins would be ruined. No, young wine must go into new wineskins. And no-one, having drunk old wine, prefers young wine; for he says, 'The old is good'."

CHAPTER 6

Now it happened that he was walking through the grainfields on a Sabbath Day, and his disciples were plucking the heads of grain, rubbing them in their hands, and eating them. Some of the Pharisees said, "Why are you doing what is unlawful on the Sabbath?"

Jesus answered them by saying, "Haven't you read what David did when he and his men were hungry? He went into the house of God, took the special bread for the offering, and ate it; and he gave some to those who were with him. And this was the bread that was unlawful to eat, except for the priests alone." He said to them, "The Son of Man is Lord of the Sabbath".

On another Sabbath Day, he went into the synagogue to teach. And a man was there with a deformed right hand. The Scribes and Pharisees were watching Jesus in case he healed on the Sabbath, so that they could accuse him.

But Jesus knew what they were thinking. He said to the man with the deformed hand, "Get up and stand here in the middle".

†   A short proverbial saying or story.

And he rose and stood there.

Jesus said to them, "Let me ask you, on the Sabbath is it lawful to do good or to do evil? To save life or destroy?" Looking round at all of them, he said to the man, "Stretch out your hand". He did so, and his hand was restored.

This made them furious, and they began to discuss with one another what they might do to Jesus.

Around that time, he went out to the mountain to pray, and spent all night in prayer to God. When it was day, he summoned his disciples, and chose twelve of them, whom he called apostles[†]. There was Simon (also called Peter), Andrew his brother, James, John, Philip, Bartholomew, Matthew, Thomas, James (son of Alphaeus), Simon (called the Zealot), Judas (son of James) and Judas Iscariot, who became a traitor.

He went down with them to a plain, along with a great crowd of his disciples. And a huge number of people from all over Judea, and Jerusalem, and the coastal region of Tyre and Sidon, came to hear him and to be healed of their diseases. Those who were troubled by unclean spirits were also being healed. The whole crowd was trying to touch him, because power was emanating from him and healing everyone.

Then he turned his attention to his disciples, and said,

"Blessed are you poor, because the kingdom of God belongs to you.

"Blessed are you who are hungry now, because you will be fed.

"Blessed are you who weep now, because you will laugh.

"Blessed are you when people hate you and ostracise you and criticise you and and blacken your name on account of the Son of Man. Rejoice and leap for joy in that day, for great is

---

† 'Apostle' literally means 'one sent out (for a task)'. In the New Testament, it usually refers to those sent out to continue Jesus' preaching.

your reward in heaven; for the fathers of those who persecute you used to do the same to the prophets.

"However, woe to you who are rich, because you are receiving your comfort.

"Woe to you who are full now, because you will be hungry.

"Woe to you who laugh now, because you will mourn and weep.

"Woe to you when everyone speaks well of you, for their fathers used to do the same to the false prophets.

"But to you who are listening, I say: Love your enemies. Do good to those who hate you. Bless those who curse you. Pray for those who mistreat you. If someone strikes you on the cheek, offer him the other cheek as well; and if someone takes your coat, let him have your shirt as well. To everyone who asks of you, give; and if someone takes your things, don't demand them back. And in the way you want people to treat you, do the same for them.

"If you love those who love you, what credit is that to you? For even the sinners love those who love them. And if you do good to those who do good to you, what credit is that to you? Even the sinners do that. And if you lend to those you know will return the favour, what credit is that to you? Even sinners lend to sinners so that they might receive as much back.

"But love your enemies, and do good and lend without expecting anything. Your reward will be great, and you will sons of the Most High[†], because he shows kindness to the ungrateful and the wicked. Be merciful, as your Father is merciful. And do not judge, or else you also will be judged. Do not condemn, or else you also will be condemned. Forgive, and you will be forgiven. Give, and it will be given to you—a good amount, pressed down, shaken and running over, will be put in your lap—for the

† To *be sons of* was a Jewish way of saying you were like someone or something; that you 'bore the family likeness'.

amount you give will be the amount you get back."

He also told them a parable: "Can the blind lead the blind? Will they not both fall into a ditch? The student[†] is not above the teacher; but everyone who has been fully trained will be like his teacher.

"Why do you notice the speck that is in your brother's eye, but do not consider the log that is in your own? How can you possibly say to your brother, 'Brother, let me take the speck out of your eye', when you haven't noticed the log in your own eye. You hypocrite! First take the log out of your own eye, and then you will be able to see clearly to remove the speck from your brother's eye.

"For a good tree never produces rotten fruit; nor does a rotten tree produce good fruit, because each tree is known by its own fruit. Figs are not gathered from thorn bushes, nor are grapes picked from bramble bushes. A good man brings out good things from the good treasure of his heart; and an evil man brings forth evil from the evil in his heart. For his mouth speaks from the overflow of the heart.

"Why do you call me 'Lord, Lord', but do not do what I say? Everyone who comes to me and hears my message and puts it into practice—let me show you what that person is like: He is like a man who was building a house, and who dug down deep and laid the foundation on solid rock. When a flood came, the river burst upon that house, but could not shake it, because the house was well built. However, the person who hears but does not put into practice is like a man who built a house on the soil, without a foundation. And when the river burst upon it, the house collapsed immediately, and was utterly ruined."

†   Literally, *disciple*.

CHAPTER 7

After Jesus had completed all his teachings in the hearing of the people, he entered Capernaum. Now a certain centurion had a highly-valued servant, who was ill to the point of death. When the centurion heard about Jesus, he sent some Jewish elders to ask him whether he could come, so that the servant might escape death.

They came to Jesus and strongly urged him, "This man is worthy of your help, for he loves our people and even built our synagogue."

So Jesus went with them. When he was not far from the house, the centurion sent friends to say to him, "Lord, do not trouble yourself, for I do not deserve to have you come under my roof. And neither did I count myself worthy to come to see you. But say the word and my servant will be healed. For I too am a man under authority, and I have soldiers under me. I say to this one, 'Go' and he goes, and to another 'Come here' and he comes, and to my servant, 'Do this', and he does it."

When he heard this, Jesus was amazed at him, and turning to the crowd that was following him, said, "I tell you, not even in Israel have I found faith such as this!"

And those who had been sent to Jesus returned to the house, and found the servant well again.

Not long afterwards, Jesus went to a city called Nain, and his disciples and a great crowd went with him. As he drew near the gate of the city, he saw that they were carrying out a dead person, who was the only son of his widowed mother. A crowd from the city was with the widow. When he saw her, the Lord had compassion for her, and said, "Don't cry". And he stepped forward and laid his hand on the coffin. The pall-bearers stood still, and he said, "Young man, I say to you, rise up!"

The dead man sat up and began to speak, and Jesus gave him

to his mother.

Fear took hold of everyone, and they glorified God, saying, "A great prophet has arisen amongst us" and "God has visited his people". And this report about him spread through all of Judea and the surrounding region.

John's disciples told him about all these things. So John selected two of his disciples, and sent them to the Lord to ask, "Are you the Coming One, or should we wait for another?" The men came to Jesus and said, "John the Baptist sent us to you to ask, 'Are you the Coming One or should we wait for another?'".

At that particular time, Jesus healed many people from illnesses and diseases and evil spirits, and he gave many blind people back their sight. He answered the men, "Go back and tell John what you see and hear: the blind see, the crippled walk, and the lepers are being cleansed; the deaf hear, the dead are being raised, and the poor are hearing the great news. And blessed is the one who does not stumble because of me."

When John's messengers had departed, he began to talk to the crowd about John, "What did you go out into the desert to see? A reed being shaken by the wind? What did you go out to see? A man dressed in fancy clothes? No, those who have gorgeous clothes and luxuries live in royal palaces. So what did you go out to see? A prophet? Yes, I tell you, and much more than a prophet. He is the one about whom it is written in the Scriptures, 'See, I send my messenger before your face, who will prepare the way before you'. I tell you, among those born of women, none is greater than John; but the person who is least in the kingdom of God is greater than John!"

(And when all the people heard this, including the tax collectors, they considered God justified, since they had been baptized with John's baptism. However, the Pharisees and religious lawyers, who had not been baptized by him, rejected God's purpose for themselves.)

"To what, then, shall I compare the people of this generation? What are they like? They are like children sitting in the market-place, calling out to one another, 'We played the flute for you and you didn't dance; we wailed and you didn't weep'. For John the Baptist came not eating bread nor drinking wine, and you say, 'He has a demon!' The Son of Man came eating and drinking, and you say, 'Look, he's a glutton and a drunkard, a friend of tax collectors and sinners'. Yet wisdom is considered justified by all her children."

One of the Pharisees invited Jesus to dine with him, and Jesus went to the Pharisee's house, and reclined at the table. Now there was a woman in the city who was a sinner, and when she found out that Jesus was having dinner at the Pharisee's house, she brought an alabaster jar of perfumed lotion. She stood behind Jesus, near his feet, crying; and her tears were wetting his feet, and she started to wipe his feet with her hair and to kiss them, and to anoint them with the lotion.

When the Pharisee who invited Jesus saw this, he said to himself, "If this man were a prophet, he would realise who she was and what kind of woman was touching him—that she is a sinner".

And Jesus answered him, "Simon, I have something to say to you".

"Teacher", he said, "go ahead and speak".

"There were two people in debt to a certain money-lender. One owed him the equivalent of 500 days wages; the other 50[†]. Neither of them were able to pay, and so the money-lender forgave both debts. Which of them, then, will love him more?"

....

†   Literally 500 denarii and 50 denarii. The denarius was a day's wage for a labourer.

Simon answered, "I suppose the one who was forgiven more".

He said to him, "You have judged rightly".

And turning to the woman, he said to Simon, "Do you see this woman? I came into your house—you did not provide water for my feet; but she has been wetting my feet with her tears and wiping them with her hair. You gave me no kiss; but from the time I arrived she has not stopped kissing my feet. You did not anoint my head with oil; but she has anointed my feet with lotion. And so I say to you, she has had many sins forgiven; thus, she loves much. But he who is forgiven little, loves little."

He said to her, "Your sins are forgiven".

And those who were reclining at the table with him, began to say to themselves, "Who is this, who even forgives sins?"

He said to the woman, "Your faith has rescued you; go in peace".

CHAPTER 8

Soon after this, he toured through the cities and towns, preaching and announcing the great news of the kingdom of God, and the twelve apostles were with him. Certain women were also with him who had been healed of evil spirits and ill-nesses—Mary who was called Magdalene (from whom seven demons had been cast out), Joanna (the wife of Herod's steward Chuza), Susanna, and many others. These women provided for them out of their own money.

A great crowd was gathering, coming to him from every city. So he told a parable:

"A sower went out to sow his seed. And while he was sowing, some of the seed fell on the path and was trampled on, and the birds ate it. Other seed fell on rocky ground, and as soon as it grew it withered, because it had no moisture. Still other seed fell in the midst of thorns, and the thorns grew up alongside, and choked it. But other seed fell on good soil, and having grown, it produced a massive crop." After saying this, he called out, "Let anyone with ears to hear, listen!"

His disciples asked him what this parable meant. He said to them, "You have been granted to know the secret of the kingdom of God, but for the rest it is all in parables, so that even though they 'see' they may not see, and even though they hear they may not understand. This is what the parable means: The seed is the message of God. The seed which fell on the path represents those who hear, but then the devil comes and takes the message from their heart, so that they may not believe and be rescued. The seed which fell on the rocky ground stands for those who, when they hear, receive the message with joy. But they do not have any root. They believe for a while, but when the time of testing comes, they pull back.

"Now the seed which fell into the thorns represents those who hear, but as they go along, they are choked by the worries and riches and pleasures of life; and they never mature to produce fruit. And the seed which fell in good soil—these are the people who hear the message, and hold onto it in their good and noble hearts, and, in persevering, produce fruit.

"No-one after lighting a lamp covers it with a bowl or puts it under the bed, but places it on a lampstand, so that those who come in might see the light. For there is nothing hidden that will not become plain, and nothing concealed that will not become known and come to light. Be careful, then, how you listen. For whoever has, more will be given to him; but whoever does not have, even what he seems to have will be taken away from him."

His mother and brothers arrived to see him, but they were not able to reach him because of the crowd. And someone told him, "Your mother and brothers are standing outside, wanting to see you". Jesus replied, "These are my mother and brothers—those who hear the message of God and put it into practice".

One day, he got into a boat with his disciples and said to them, "Let us go across to the other side of the lake". They set out, and while they were sailing, he fell asleep. Then a windstorm came down the lake. The boat was filling with water and they were in real danger.

They went and woke Jesus and said, "Master, Master, we are about to die!" But he got up and rebuked the wind and the raging water. And they stopped, and it became calm.

He said to the disciples, "Where is your faith?" They were afraid and astonished, and said to one another, "Who then is this, that he commands even the winds and the water, and they obey him?"

They sailed on to the country of the Gerasenes, which is on the shore opposite Galilee. When he got out of the boat, he was met by a certain man from the city, who had demons. For a long time he had not worn clothes, and he lived among the tombs rather than in a house.

When he saw Jesus, he cried out and fell down before him, and said in a loud voice, "What have I got to do with you, Jesus, son of the Most High God? I beg you, do not torment me." For he had commanded the unclean spirit to come out of the man. Many times it had seized him, and he used to be bound with chains and shackles, and kept under guard. But he would break the bonds, and be driven by the demon into the desert.

Jesus asked him, "What is your name?" And he replied, "Legion", because many demons had gone into him. And they pleaded with him not to order them to depart into the abyss.

Now there was a good-sized herd of pigs grazing on the hillside; and the demons begged him to permit them to enter the pigs, and he allowed them to do so. The demons left the man and went into the pigs, and the herd rushed over the cliff into the lake and was drowned.

When those who were looking after the pigs saw this, they fled, and reported it to those in the city and in the country, who then came out to see what had happened. They came to Jesus and found the man from whom the demons had been driven out sitting at Jesus' feet, clothed and in his right mind. And they were afraid. Those who had seen it all, explained how the demon-possessed man had been rescued[†].

Then all those from the region of the Gerasenes asked him to go away from them, for they were gripped with great fear. And getting back into the boat, he returned.

The man from whom the demons had come out begged to go with him, but Jesus sent him away, saying, "Go back to your home, and tell what God has done for you". And he went through the whole city, declaring what Jesus had done for him.

When Jesus returned, a crowd was there to welcome him, for they had all been waiting for him. A man named Jairus, who was a ruler of the synagogue, came straight up to Jesus and fell at his feet, and begged him to come to his house. The reason was that his only daughter, who was about twelve years old, was dying.

While he was on his way, the crowds almost crushed him. Among them was a woman who had suffered from a flow of blood for twelve years, and no-one had been able to cure her, though she had spent all her resources on doctors. Coming up behind Jesus, she touched the fringe of his clothes, and immediately the flow of blood ceased.

Jesus said, "Who touched me?" They all denied it, and Peter

---

†   Or *saved,* or *healed,* also below.

said, "Master, the crowds are pressing in and crushing you".

But Jesus said, "Someone touched me, for I know that power has gone out from me".

When the woman saw that she could not hide, she came trembling and fell down before him. And she declared before everyone why she had touched him, and how she had been instantly healed.

He said to her, "Daughter, your faith has rescued you. Go in peace."

While he was still speaking, someone came from the synagogue ruler's house and said to Jairus, "Your daughter is dead. Do not trouble the teacher any longer."

Jesus heard this, and said to him, "Don't be afraid; only have faith and she will be rescued".

When he came to the house, he let no-one go in with him except Peter, James and John, and the girl's father and mother. Everyone was weeping and mourning for her, but he said, "Do not weep. For she is not dead, only sleeping." And they laughed at him, because they knew she had died.

Jesus grasped her hand, and called out, "Child, rise up!"

And her spirit returned and she sat up immediately; and he ordered that she be given something to eat.

Her parents were astounded, and he commanded them not to say what had happened.

CHAPTER 9

He called together the twelve, and gave them power and authority over all the demons, and to heal sicknesses. And he sent them out to proclaim the kingdom of God and to heal the sick. He said to them, "Take nothing for the journey—no staff, no bag, no bread, no money, not even a spare shirt. And whatever house you enter, stay there, and leave from there. Wherever they do not welcome you, shake the dust off your feet as you leave that city, as a testimony to them."

They set out, and went through the towns announcing the great news and healing everywhere.

Now Herod the tetrarch heard about all these happenings. He was perplexed, because it was being said by some that John had been raised from the dead, and by others that Elijah had appeared; and others were saying that an ancient prophet had risen up.

Herod said, "John I beheaded; but who is this man I am hearing these things about?" And he tried to see him.

When the apostles returned, they reported to Jesus what they had done. And taking them with him, he withdrew privately to a city called Bethsaida.

But the crowds found out, and followed him. He welcomed them, and spoke to them about the kingdom of God, and cured those who were in need of healing. The day was drawing to a close, and the twelve came and said to him, "Send the crowd away, so that they can go into the surrounding towns and fields to lodge, and to find food—for this place is a desert."

But Jesus said to them, "Give them something to eat yourselves". They said, "We don't have more than five loaves of bread and two fish; unless perhaps we should go and buy provisions for all these people!" (For there were about 5000 men).

He said to his disciples, "Sit them down in groups of 50". And they did so, and the crowd all sat down.

Taking the five loaves and two fish, Jesus looked up to heaven, blessed them, broke them, and kept giving them to the disciples to set before the crowd.

And they ate and were all satisfied. The leftovers were gathered up, and there were twelve baskets of pieces.

Once while he was praying alone, with his disciples close by, he asked them a question: "Who do the crowds say that I am?"

And they answered, "John the Baptist; others say Elijah, and others that an ancient prophet has risen up".

He said to them, "And you, who do you say I am?"

Peter answered, "The Christ of God".

And he sternly commanded them not to say this to anyone, saying, "The Son of Man must suffer much, and be rejected by the elders and Chief Priests and scribes, and be killed, and on the third day be raised up."

He said to them all, "If anyone wants to come after me, let him deny himself and pick up his cross each day, and follow me. For whoever wants to save his life will lose it; but whoever loses his life for my sake—he will save it. For what profit does a person get if he gains the whole world, but loses or forfeits his very self? For whoever is ashamed of me and my words, the Son of Man will be ashamed of him when he comes in his glory and in the glory of the Father and the holy angels. I tell you the truth, there are some standing here who will not taste death until they see the kingdom of God."

CHAPTER 4

JESUS' SURNAME

In Martin Scorceses' film, *The Last Temptation of Christ*, Jesus is cast as a passionate, though sexually repressed, prophet. In Barbara Thiering's best-selling book, *Jesus the Man*, Jesus is portrayed as a married-with-three-kids-then-divorced Jewish teacher. Stained-glass windows often portray him as an angelic, one-dimensional zombie. Extreme right-wing American politicians uphold him as the champion of their quasi-religious racist and bigoted views (which is pretty ironic considering Jesus was a dark-skinned Jew). Hollywood dresses him up in a nighty and secures him a place among the irrelevant relics of the past. And the Mambo clothing label has painted him as a thong-wearing, beer-drinking, cricket-watching Aussie. The list goes on and on.

It seems that everyone has their own version of Jesus. It's as if he's become an icon, symbolising whatever it is about ourselves we want to promote or justify. But most of these Jesus-icons are nine-parts imagination and one-part reality. Compared with the man described in the original documents, they prove to be little more than a series of guesses and wishful thoughts.

Who exactly was Jesus? To take us back to the Joe Louis analogy, what is written on Jesus' business card?

The simplest way to answer this question is to begin with the strange, though prestigious, title bestowed on Jesus at his birth. All the biographers agree that this particular title best captures Jesus' true identity.

The first time we come across the title is from the lips of the angelic messenger who explained to some very frightened shepherds that the newly arrived baby up there in the animals feeding trough (traditionally called a 'manger') was someone very special indeed:

> *As it happened, while they were there in Bethlehem, the time came for her to have the baby, and she gave birth to her firstborn son. And because there was no room for them in the inn, she used strips of cloth to wrap him up, and a food trough for his cradle.*
>
> *In that part of the country, there were shepherds who stayed out in the fields at night to keep watch over their flock. Without warning, one of the Lord's angelic Messengers appeared to them, and the brilliance of the Lord shone all around them. They were terrified, but the Messenger said to them, "Do not be afraid. Listen, I am here to bring you news of great joy which is for all the people: today, a saviour has been born to you in the city of David. He is Christ, the Lord. (Luke 2:6-11)*[†]

Growing up in a religion-less home, I had no idea what the word 'Christ' meant. I assumed it must have been Jesus' surname. Just as I'm John *Dickson*, he was Jesus *Christ* and his parents were Mary and Joseph Christ, and then Grandpa

[†] The references in this book to parts of Luke's biography use the standard numbering system of chapters and verses that was developed in the mid-16th century.

Christ, and so on. Then someone very kindly explained that 'Christ' was in fact a title, like King or Prime Minister. It was the greatest of all titles, and one with a long and important history. Without turning this into a history lesson, let me briefly explain.

For the thousand years before the birth of Jesus, the kings who ruled Israel (Jesus' homeland) were viewed as the representatives of the Creator himself. It was reasoned that since God was THE KING of the universe, any earthly king who ruled with God's blessing was somehow the Almighty's right-hand man, deriving his authority to govern directly from God. To reinforce this idea, an elaborate coronation ceremony developed in which a prophet or priest would fill a huge jar with fine Middle Eastern olive oil and pour it over the head of the king-to-be, until he was drenched from tip to toe. As messy as it must have been, this *anointing* ceremony was a way of symbolising God endowing the king with authority to rule on his behalf.

Reflecting on this ceremony the prophets of the Old Testament (the first half of the Bible) predicted that one day God would send a truly anointed king, someone who would be endowed not symbolically with olive oil but literally with divine authority to speak and act on the Almighty's behalf. This person would teach and embody all that the Creator wanted us to know about himself and about our relationship to him. It was quite a job description. Not surprisingly, this future leader came to be spoken of as the 'Anointed One', which in Hebrew is translated by the word 'Messiah' and in Greek (the language of the New Testament) is translated by the word 'Christos', or as we write it in English, 'Christ'. In other words, the term 'Christ' was anything but a surname.

It was a title reserved for the king who would one day come, in fulfillment of ancient prophecies, to speak and act for the Almighty himself.

[The Old Testament contains quite a number of predictions about the coming king or Christ. If you are interested in reading some of these I've included them in the 'Extra Information' section at the back of the book. You can find them at page 211.]

The significance of the title 'the Christ' cannot easily be exaggerated. When the angel told the shepherds that the Christ had arrived, this was news of extraordinary importance. It meant that a thousand years of waiting was over. It meant that, finally, all that God wanted to say and display to the men and women of the world would become a reality in the words and actions of this remarkable individual.

It is important for our appreciation of Luke's account of Jesus' life to know that many Jews of this period put a decidedly political and/or military spin on the role they expected the Anointed One (or 'Christ') to fulfill. For generations, the Jewish people had been dominated by foreign powers who saw the land of Palestine as a highly significant trade and military route between the Mediterranean and Egypt and the rest of North Africa. At the time of Jesus, the Jews suffered the indignity of being ruled and occupied by the greatest military machine of ancient times, the Roman Empire. The Romans allowed some semblance of Jewish life for the people of Palestine, but the severe taxes, numerous garrison towns and constant flow of armed soldiers in the city streets were a constant reminder that their beloved 'promised land' was, in fact, the property of a Roman Emperor, sitting in a palace thousands of kilometres away. In such a context, it is understandable that when Jewish people talked to each other about the arrival of the promised Christ—the one who would speak and act for God—high on their wish list of things for him to achieve was the destruction of the Romans, and the liberation of their nation.

But one of the striking things about Jesus' ownership of the title is that he refused to give it any political or military connotations at all. He came to speak and act for God, but not precisely in the way one might have expected. In fact, some of the things he did as the Christ ran absolutely counter to popular expectations about his role.

How exactly Jesus did choose to display his authority as the Christ is a central concern of Luke's biography, especially in these opening chapters. Let me describe some of them in detail.

SPEAKING
GOD'S WORDS

In chapter four Luke recounts an episode in which Christ's authority to speak on God's behalf is dramatically highlighted. Jesus is now a grown man, about thirty years old (the age when Jewish men were allowed to begin teaching publicly). According to Luke, one of Jesus' first public announcements was made in his home town of Nazareth, a small town in the north of Palestine. It was normal practice in the synagogue (Jewish church) of this time for someone to read aloud from the Scriptures and then to make some comments on the meaning and importance of the particular passage. The modern practice of a 'sermon' in church actually derives from this custom. Anyway, on this particular occasion the Scripture reading and 'sermon' were given to Jesus, and what he said about the passage and about himself left everyone dumbfounded. Here's Luke's account again:

He stood up to read, and the scroll of the prophet Isaiah was handed to him. Unrolling it, he found the place where it was written,

"The Spirit of the Lord is upon me, because he has anointed me to announce great news to the poor; he has sent me to proclaim release for prisoners, and sight once

more for the blind, to send the oppressed away free; to pro-claim the acceptable year of the Lord".

Rolling up the scroll, he gave it to the assistant and sat down. And the eyes of everyone in the synagogue were fixed on him.

He began to speak to them, "Today, this Scripture is fulfilled in your hearing". (Luke 4:17-21)

The passage Jesus read aloud in the synagogue that day came from a biblical book written hundreds of years before by the prophet Isaiah. Isaiah was one of the prophets I mentioned earlier who predicted a great many things about the arrival of the 'Anointed One'. This particular passage (found in chapter 61 of the book of Isaiah) foretells the appearance of the one 'anointed' to speak God's mind.

The people in the audience that day probably expected Jesus merely to make a few comments about how fantastic it will be when the Anointed One spoken of in Isaiah arrives and tells us things that only God himself could reveal. In fact, the Dead Sea Scrolls (Jewish documents written just prior to Jesus' birth and found only 50 years ago) contain a number of mini-sermons on this same passage, and they do precisely that.

But Jesus does not simply comment upon the meaning and importance of the passage. He states emphatically that this prophecy, written centuries before, was all about him: "Today this scripture is fulfilled in your hearing". According to Jesus, *he* is the preacher 'anointed' to speak God's mind, to say the things only God could say. Hearing him teach was hearing the voice of God himself. It is a very, very big claim, and it's no wonder that all the people in the audience were, as Luke records, "amazed at the gracious words that came from his mouth".

There are so many voices in our world (as there were in the ancient world too) scrambling for our attention and allegiance. Advertisers tell us what to buy in order to be happy. Politicians inform us how to vote in order to be well governed. TV shows and magazines tell us how to dress in order to be noticed. Therapists and popular authors tell us how to behave in order to have healthy, happy families and careers. The range of voices is endless. It is so difficult even to keep abreast of the mass of competing information out there, let alone to assess its truthfulness and value for our lives. If only we could hear a reliable voice above all the 'noise'; a voice that brought clarity to our busy and complex lives, one that offered a dose of reality in the midst of the triviality of much of our media driven society. The claim of Luke, the claim of Christianity, is that just such a voice can be heard in the words of the Christ himself, Jesus of Nazareth, the one 'anointed' to speak on God's behalf. Throughout the rest of Luke's biography you'll have ample opportunity to hear that voice loud and clear.

CHAPTER 6

MENDING THE BROKENNESS

Another aspect of Jesus' authority as the Christ that Luke emphasises is his work as a healer of physical ailments. So, for instance, he reports:

> *Jesus stood up and left the synagogue, and went to Simon's house. Simon's mother-in-law was in the grip of a high fever, and they asked him to do something for her.*
>
> *Jesus stood over her and rebuked the fever, and it left her. She got straight up and began to serve them.*
>
> *As the sun was setting, everyone who had any who were sick with various diseases brought them to him. He laid his hands on each one of them, and healed them. (Luke 4:38-40)*

As scientifically distasteful as talk of 'miraculous healings' may be to some modern, Western minds, there is no avoiding the fact that all of the biographies of Jesus agree that he was renowned for an ability to mend the physical (as well as spiritual) brokenness of countless individuals he came across.

It might be tempting to dismiss Jesus' healings as the foolish talk of a culture that knew nothing about medical science. Now that we know about physiology and medicine (the argument goes), we can explain away this talk of people being 'miraculously' healed. But the reality is that the people of this era did know about physiology and medicine. Indeed, as I said before, Luke was a medical doctor himself. He knew well the reality and benefits of 'physical' cures. Nevertheless, he is adamant that the activity of Jesus fell into an entirely different category and was on a scale way beyond that which could be explained naturalistically.[†]

So difficult were Jesus' activities to explain that the reports about them made their way into non-Christian writings of the period. As we saw earlier, Josephus, the Jewish historian, states that Jesus was a "man who performed startling feats". More significant is the critical statement against Jesus in the official Jewish education document (the Talmud) deriving from the second century, in which Jesus is said to have "practiced sorcery". What is fascinating is that this document makes no attempt to deny the miracles of Jesus, just to reinterpret them in an unfavourable light. This doesn't 'prove' that Jesus did miracles, but it is good evidence that his activities were of such a nature and of such renown that even a century after his death the general non-Christian populace still believed he performed feats which required 'miraculous' explanations.

A friend of mine who is Professor of Medicine at the University of Western Australia had this to say about Jesus' healings when I asked him recently what he made of them:

A couple of things strike me about Jesus' healing miracles. First is their magnitude—withered hands were restored, eyes that had never worked started to work. That means that tissue such as skin cells, muscles, nerves, retinal cells,

†   For a full-scale historical and philosophical analysis of the reality of Jesus' healings by a leading New Testament historian, see G. H. Twelftree, *Jesus: the miracle worker*, IVP, Illinois, 1999.

*and the like were recreated. And then they were made to work; the brain cells controlling them/responding to them were somehow re-organized. These events were not mere 'backaches that disappear with suggestion'; they were serious creative events. The fact that Jesus' opponents got angry only over **when** he did them (on the Sabbath rest-day) and in whose name he did them, rather than **whether** he did them, suggests that they were not able to say "ha! that was just an illusion". Obviously the limbs and eyes did work or they wouldn't have gotten angry in this way.*

Secondly, speaking as a scientist and clinician, Jesus' healings tell me about the God who originally created the 'stuff' of the universe… The miracles of Jesus display the same creative power. And, interestingly, God did both creative acts for the same reason—not for fun or as a party trick or so that we could see how clever he was, but as an act of love. He made the universe because he wanted a place in which we could live and be loved by him as his children; he healed sick people through Jesus' ministry because he was moved with precisely the same fatherly compassion.

Prof. Bruce W. S. Robinson
MBBS MD FRACP FRCP DTM&H FCCP
Professor of Medicine, University of Western Australia.

Luke would agree: Jesus' healings were not the work of a magician or sorcerer. They were signs of God's desire to mend the brokenness of the world through the one he sent to speak and act on his behalf: the Christ.

CHAPTER 7

FORGIVENESS ON OFFER

For me, the most significant aspect of Jesus' authority as the Christ was not his teaching (as striking as this was), nor his healings (as amazing as these were), but his claim to have the authority to hand out God's forgiveness to whomever he wanted. On one occasion, he chose to emphasize this point in a way he knew would land himself in trouble with the religious leaders of his day (though he seemed not to worry too much about upsetting religious leaders).

One day, Jesus was teaching, and some Pharisees[†] and teachers of the law were sitting there. They had come from all the towns of Galilee and Judea and Jerusalem. And the power of the Lord was with him to heal.

Some men arrived carrying a paralysed man on a stretcher. They were trying to bring him in to put him before Jesus, but because of the crowd, they could find no way through. They went up onto the roof of the house, and lowered him down on his stretcher through the tiles, right into their midst in front of Jesus. When Jesus saw their faith, he said, "Friend, your sins are forgiven".

The scribes and Pharisees began to think to themselves, "Who is this who speaks such blasphemies? Who is able to forgive sins except God alone?" (Luke 5:17-21)

----

† A strict religious group among the Jews.

The amazing thing about this episode is not the adventurous way these friends got Jesus' attention, though Jesus does appear to be impressed. It's not even that Jesus went on to heal the disabled man. The truly incredible thing is that Jesus publicly claimed to be able to forgive people for the things they had done to offend God himself—their 'sins'. This is an extraordinary claim.

Imagine I stole your car, then, feeling guilty about it, decided to return the vehicle to one of your friends who promptly announced, "That's OK, I forgive you". How would you react? Surely you would feel upset and a little cheated, not only by me for stealing the car but also by your friend for presuming to be able to forgive me on your behalf. No-one has the right to hand out your forgiveness but you alone! Surely it would be the same with God. How on earth could a mere mortal presume to forgive another human being for the things they'd done to offend the Almighty?

The religious leaders there that day—the Pharisees and teachers of the law—picked up on this point and thought to themselves, "Who is this who speaks such blasphemies? Who is able to forgive sins except God alone?" They reasoned that Jesus' claim to be able to forgive this man was tantamount to claiming God's authority for himself. Technically, this is 'blasphemy', and in the culture of that day—as with some cultures today—blasphemy is punishable by death.

At this point, Jesus could easily have 'qualified' his statement by explaining that all he meant to say was, "I tell you that God forgives your sins". But far from backtracking, Jesus takes the opportunity to emphasize publicly that God had in fact authorized him, as the Christ, to offer forgiveness to anyone he chose. The story continues:

> *But Jesus realised what they were thinking, and answered them, "Why do you think this way in your hearts? Which is easier: to say, 'Your sins are forgiven' or to say, 'Get up and walk'? But so that you may know that the son of man has authority on earth to forgive sins..." He said to the paralysed man, "I tell you, get up, and pick up your stretcher and go back to your home".*
>
> *And immediately he got up right there in front of them, picked up what he was lying on and went back to his home, giving honour and praise to God.*
>
> *Everybody was stunned, and honoured God. They were quite afraid, and said, "We have seen extraordinary things today". (Luke 5:22-26)*

In some ways, the healing of the disabled man was incidental, although I'm sure it was a delight for the man himself. On this occasion, the healing was more than just an act of kindness on the part of Christ. It was a *visible* sign that Jesus could also do the *invisible* miracle of handing out God's forgiveness; that he could literally look men and women in the eye and say, "All that you've done to offend God, I here and now forgive, with all of God's authority". It is no wonder the crowd there that day were "stunned" and said to one another, "We have seen extraordinary things today".

Life can be very unforgiving at times. People we've hurt can hold grudges against us to their deathbed. A small slip-up at work can mean the difference between a promotion and redundancy. An angry word can cause a divide between husbands and wives, or between parents and their children, that fails to resolve for years to come, if at all. Into just such a

world, Jesus came and announced that despite the unforgiving nature of much of our society, God was in the business
of offering people a clean slate, and he had authorized his
Christ to publicise and make good that offer.

CHAPTER 8

THE QUESTION OF LEADERSHIP

Perhaps the most awkward aspect of Jesus' authority as the Christ (at least for us) was his insistence that men and women adopt his agenda over their own; or in other words, to follow him as their leader. It must have been inspiring to hear him speak with such elegance and majesty; it must have been exciting to watch him mend the broken lives of the ill; it must have been comforting to hear him extend God's forgiveness to those around him. But how must it have felt to have this man walk up to you one day and say, "I want you to follow my lead from now on!"?

> *After this, Jesus went out and saw a tax collector named Levi sitting at the tax collecting booth. He said to him, "Follow me", and he got up, left everything, and followed him. (Luke 5:27-28)*

Tax collectors in this culture were not the conservative, respectable, suit-wearing men and women of our modern tax office. They were very often wealthy, unscrupulous and decidedly unreligious businessmen who made their living by extracting taxes from their fellow-countrymen on behalf of the hated Romans, and then creaming money off the top to keep for themselves. Following anyone else's agenda, let alone that of someone like Jesus, was under normal circumstances the last thing on a tax collector's mind. But along comes Jesus one day, with a simple 'follow me', and everything changes.

It is difficult to know exactly what motivated Levi to drop everything and follow Christ. Perhaps he'd heard him preach before and had been struck by the clarity and reality of his words. Perhaps he'd just heard the rumours about one who could heal the sick and hand out God's mercy to all. Whatever Levi's reasons, his soul was captivated by Jesus' challenge.

Luke's biography contains many, many examples of individuals like Levi—the irreligious and religious alike—who hear Jesus' demand to follow him and find themselves caught up in an entirely new life agenda. In fact, Luke's presentation of Jesus appears to move deliberately in this direction. It's as if Luke wants his readers to realise that Jesus' authority as the Christ was not an intangible, distant reality—as if his life were a travelling circus we could enjoy from our seats—but one that touched human lives personally and individually.

I should probably add that, despite our modern assumptions to the contrary, taking up Christ's agenda did not mark the end of a person's freedom and fulfillment, and the beginning of a one-dimensional, slave-like existence. Far from it. Although Levi's decision to accept Christ's challenge would have meant some significant life changes—probably some quite difficult ones—it's worth pointing out that his first step in this new adventure was to throw a party for all his friends and associates, with Christ as the guest of honour.

And Levi held a great feast for Jesus at his house, with a large crowd of tax collectors; and others were there as well, reclining at the table with them.

Now the Pharisees and Scribes complained to his disciples, "Why do you eat and drink with tax collectors and sinners?" (Luke 5:29-30)

According to this paragraph, if anyone's agenda was 'one-dimensional', it was that of the religious establishment, the Pharisees and teachers of the law (or Scribes), not Jesus. Jesus' agenda was something worth celebrating.

Christ's captivating power to call on people to live by his agenda was not only an ancient phenomenon. Today, millions upon millions of people from 2,197 different language groups have heard the unsettling though exciting words 'Follow me', and have found themselves irresistibly drawn to do just that.

CHAPTER 9

†RUE CONFESSIONS

I said before that Luke appears to have organized his biography in a way that encourages the reader to realise that Jesus' authority as the Christ affected people personally. This is nowhere more apparent than in the first climax of his biography in chapter nine.

The account of Christ's activities from chapter four through to nine covers the first year and a half of his public life. In another 18 months or so his actions would wind him up in serious trouble with the political and religious authorities of his day. Right in the middle of this three-year public career, a very significant event occurred: Jesus put his colleagues on the spot by asking them who they believed him to be.

> *Once while he was praying alone, with his disciples close by, he asked them a question: "Who do the crowds say that I am?"*
>
> *And they answered, "John the Baptist; others say Elijah, and others that an ancient prophet has risen up".*
>
> *He said to them, "And you, who do you say I am?"*
>
> *Peter answered, "The Christ of God". (Luke 9:18-20)*

As readers we've known from the beginning that Jesus is the Christ but, as you may have noticed, Jesus has not yet formally claimed this title for himself. Instead, he appears almost to have avoided it, probably for fear that the political connotations of the term 'Christ' for many first-century Jews may only have encouraged a militaristic fervour against the Romans, and even started a kind of 'holy war'. This is something Jesus was not at all interested in doing. Nevertheless, Jesus' public silence about his identity appears to have led to some vigorous guesswork on the part of the crowds. Some confused him with John the Baptist, another recent man of God. Others thought he stood in the tradition of one of the great prophets of the past.

No one had had greater opportunity to put two and two together than Jesus' colleagues, or 'disciples'. And so when he turned to them and asked, "Who do you say I am?", the disciple named Peter answered with great simplicity, and no doubt a high degree of reverence too. After everything he had seen over the last year or so—Jesus' authority to speak for God, to heal diseases, to forgive people's past, and to call on people to follow his agenda—there was no other conclusion. This had to be the one. This had to be "the Christ of God".

If Luke's biography were a feature film, this moment (somewhere in the middle of the story) would be accompanied by the movie's theme music at full force and volume. The audience may even applaud out of a sense of 'arrival'. Finally, someone had discovered the truth of Jesus' identity. He is the promised Christ.

But the dramatic moment would be short-lived, for, according to Luke, no sooner does Peter arrive at the correct conclusion about Jesus' status than Jesus himself sounds a very discordant tone.

And he sternly commanded them not to say this to anyone,
saying, "The son of man must suffer much, and be rejected
by the elders and Chief Priests and scribes, and be killed,
and on the third be raised up." (Luke 9:21-22)

As I mentioned earlier, Jewish people in this period expected the Christ to arrive with power to conquer the Romans and establish God's kingdom on earth, with Israel at the centre of the action. Like his contemporaries, Peter too would have held out such hopes. But Jesus would not allow such a politicization of his role as the Christ, even for a moment. Instead, as soon as his colleagues acknowledge him as the promised Christ, he immediately informs them that his mission as the Christ does not involve conquering and crushing the national enemies of Israel, but suffering and dying at the hands of Israel's own religious and political leadership. The Christ's 'throne', if you can call it that, would be made of two large pieces of wood upon which he would be nailed. This news would have been quite a shock to his associates.

Jesus had already chosen to reveal his authority in non-military forms: he taught rather than rallied forces; he healed rather than conquered; and he forgave rather than exacted judgment. This should have given away the fact that his leadership was of a completely different kind to that normally experienced in the ancient (and modern) world. He had not come to reign like a tyrant but to restore men and women to the fullness of life intended for them by their Maker. Now, in Jesus' explanation to his disciples of why he had come, he makes it crystal clear that this mission of restoration would be achieved only at the expense of his own life.

Why exactly Jesus' mission demanded his own suffering and death becomes a major theme of Luke's biography from this point on, and will be dealt with at a later point in the book. For now it is worth simply pondering for ourselves Jesus' pointed question to his colleagues: "Who do you say I am?"

CHAPTER 10

FLATTERING MISCONCEPTIONS

I said earlier that many people hold in their minds their own version of Christ. It is as if he has become an abstract work of art, and we as the critics attempt to derive our own private meaning from the vague and ambiguous contours of his life.

Some people interpret Christ's life in a highly critical way—Melbourne academic Peter Singer, for instance, accuses Jesus of condoning cruelty to animals based on Luke 8:32-33. But most of us hold quite positive, even flattering, interpretations of Jesus. I was recently involved in a discussion about Christ's life on the ABC radio station Triple J, and I was amazed just how many of those who called in to make a comment held Jesus in great esteem. They lavished compliments on him like, the 'greatest teacher ever', the 'model of love', the 'great rebel against organized religion', an 'inspiring leader', a 'defender of the powerless', and so on. I sat there in the studio thinking, "Who would ever have thought that Jesus was such a celebrity here in a seemingly unreligious country like ours?"

These compliments reminded me of the popular views of Jesus in his own day. When Jesus asked his followers, "Who do the crowds say that I am?" they replied, "John the Baptist; others say Elijah; and others that an ancient prophet has risen up."

Each of these opinions was quite flattering, since John the Baptist, Elijah, and the rest, were great heroes of Israel's past. Associating Jesus with such great names was probably, in the minds of the crowds, something of a compliment.

But flattering misconceptions can be every bit as much a hindrance to understanding Christianity as some of the more insulting ones. They allow us to keep our distance from Christianity without actually offending the memory of Christ himself. They are a kind of religious equivalent to the romantic, "I just want to be friends!". If you've ever had this said to you, you'll know very well that it is usually just a way for someone to avoid getting close to you without causing too much offence.

There are many examples of this I-just-want-to-be-friends attitude toward Christ. In Islam, Jesus is seen as a 'prophet'. On the face of it, this is quite a positive picture. But in reality it means that Jesus is relegated by Muslims to a long list of prophets who are all made redundant by the arrival of their own prophet, Mohamed, 500 years after Christ. Again, in New-Age philosophy, Jesus is thought of as a truly 'enlightened' man, but in doing so, new-agers are able to place Christ on the shelf next to a thousand other 'enlightened ones' in the huge new-age supermarket of ideas.

Some of our own, less religious, compliments have the same effect. By calling Jesus a 'great teacher' we often relegate his significance to the realm of ethics, as if he came just to give us a list of dos and don'ts for happy living. In calling Jesus a 'great rebel against organized religion', we all too easily find our excuse for never going to church to hear any more about him. Very few people ever reject Jesus outright, but we're pretty good at saying we 'just want to be friends', and no more.

FLATTERING MISCONCEPTIONS

The other thing about these complimentary views of Jesus is that they can make us think that our response to him is an adequate one. But if Jesus really is the Christ—the one who speaks and acts for the Creator himself—calling him a 'great teacher', an 'inspiring leader' or a 'model of love' is hardly the appropriate response. It would be like responding to a life-saver who had just rescued me from certain drowning with the words, "You're a jolly good swimmer, aren't you!" On the face of it, this is a compliment, but it is hardly adequate.

A friend recently told me about a couple she knows who own an exclusive jewellery store in Sydney. One day, while the wife was attending the shop, a mild-mannered American gen-tleman walked into the shop looking to buy a pink Argyle diamond, worth $20,000 or more, for his wife. Luckily they happened to have just the item he was after. As the credit card transaction was being made, the shop's computer froze. The man lent over the counter, asked her a few questions about the operating system, and made some suggestions to get the system up and running again. Sure enough, the computer began to work again. The woman responded, "You know a bit about computers do you?", to which he nodded and said, "Yes, a little". He walked out of the shop with his diamond. Later when the woman's husband arrived at the shop, he asked how the sales had been for the day. When she explained that she had sold a pink Argyle diamond to an American, he was intrigued to find out who the man was. Looking through the transaction records he found the receipt and was surprised to discover that they had sold the diamond to a Mr Bill Gates, CEO of Microsoft. The woman felt a little silly when she remembered what she had said to him: "You know a bit about computers do you?". In reality, this is the man who practically sets the agenda for the computer industry worldwide.

Some of us do a similar thing with Christ. We 'compliment' him with the opinion that he 'knows a bit about life'. In reality, though, if Luke is to be believed, Jesus is the one God sent into the world to set the agenda for human life. He is the Christ.

When Jesus asked, "Who do you say I am?", you can be sure he wasn't fishing for compliments. He was asking those around him to search their hearts and intellects, evaluate all that they had seen, and arrive at the appropriate conclusion. To recall the Joe Louis incident, the nine chapters of Luke we've read so far function as a kind of business card for Jesus. Luke hands it to us, his readers, and awaits our response.

PART THREE

SEARCH AND RESCUE

Few images in recent times have been more deeply branded into the Australian memory than the startling survival and rescue of Stuart Diver during the 1998 Thredbo landslide disaster. After days of waiting, as we sat pinned in front of our TVs, news broke that one of the rescuers had heard a man's voice from beneath the tons of mud, rock, concrete and pieces of broken buildings. Rescuers worked frantically for the next several hours to cut a hole through the debris to free the man. All the while, the rescuer who first discovered Diver remained in constant voice contact with him, chatting with him, reassuring him, and forming a vital link between Diver himself and the hundreds of other rescue workers. Many of us will never forget that incredible moment of relief and joy when, eventually, Diver was pulled up out of the hole and into public view. As he was taken by stretcher up the hill to the ambulance, the large crowds of rescuers and onlookers cheered and applauded. Many a tear was shed that day.

Rescue! Few things are more tense, emotional and exhilarating than a man or woman, in the face of certain disaster, being saved.

At its core, the story of Christianity is one of rescue. And Christ appears at the centre of the story as the heroic rescuer. What, exactly, men and women needed rescuing from, and how Jesus came to achieve it, is a significant theme in Luke's biography from chapters ten through to nineteen. Watch out for these themes as Luke picks up the story.

LUKE'S BIOGRAPHY
Chapters 9–19

CHAPTER 9 (CONT.)

About eight days after he had said these things, Jesus took Peter, John and James up to the mountain to pray. As he was praying, the appearance of his face changed, and his clothing became white like lightning. Suddenly two men were there speaking with him—Moses and Elijah. They appeared in brilliant glory, and spoke about his departure†, which he was about to complete in Jerusalem.

Now Peter and those with him were drowsy with sleep, but they woke up and saw his glory, and the two men who were standing with him. And when they were starting to separate from Jesus to leave, Peter said to him, "Master, it is good that we are here. Let us make three tents—one for you, and one for Moses, and one for Elijah". (He didn't know what he was saying.)

While Peter was still saying this, a cloud came and surrounded them. They were afraid as they entered the cloud, and a voice came from out of the cloud and said, "This is my chosen Son; listen to him".

And when the voice had spoken, Jesus was found alone. They kept quiet and told no-one at that time about anything that they had seen.

The next day, after they had come down from the mountain, a great crowd was there to meet him. A man from the crowd cried

† Literally, *his exodus*.

out, "Teacher, I beg you to look at my son, because he is my only child. A spirit keeps on seizing him; it suddenly calls out and throws him into convulsions, with foaming at the mouth. It is destroying him, and hardly ever leaves him. I pleaded with your disciples to cast it out, but they were not able to."

Jesus answered, "O faithless and perverse generation, how long do I have to be with you and put up with you? Bring your son here."

While the boy was still coming forward, the demon attacked him and threw him into convulsions. But Jesus rebuked the unclean spirit and healed the boy, and returned him to his father.

They were all amazed at the majesty of God. But while they were marvelling at all the things he was doing, he said to his disciples, "Let this sink in: the Son of Man is about to be betrayed into the hands of men". They didn't understand this; indeed it was hidden from them so that they didn't perceive it. And they were afraid to ask him what he meant.

Now a discussion arose among them as to which of them was the greatest. Knowing what they were thinking, Jesus took a child and stood him by his side. He said to the disciples, "Whoever welcomes this child in my name, welcomes me; and whoever welcomes me, welcomes the One who sent me. For he who is least among you all is the greatest."

John replied, "Master, we saw someone casting out demons in your name, and we stopped him, because he was not following with us".

But Jesus said to him, "Don't stop him. For whoever is not against you is for you."

Jesus Begins his Final Journey, South to Jerusalem
When the time was drawing near for him to be taken up, he set himself to go to Jerusalem. He sent messengers to go before him,

and they went into a Samaritan[†] town to prepare for his arrival. The Samaritans, however, would not welcome him, because he had set himself to go to Jerusalem.

When the disciples James and John saw this, they said, "Lord, do you want us to call fire down from heaven and destroy them?" But Jesus turned and rebuked them; and they went into another town.

As they went on their way, a certain man said to him, "I will follow you wherever you go".

But Jesus said to him, "Foxes have holes, and birds have nests, but the Son of Man has nowhere to lay his head".

Jesus said to someone else, "Follow me". But he replied, "Lord, first allow me to go and bury my father".

Jesus said to him, "Let the dead bury their own dead; but you go and proclaim the kingdom of God".

Someone else also said to him, "I will follow you, Lord, but first allow me to say goodbye to my family".

Jesus replied, "No-one who puts his hand to the plough and looks back is fit for the kingdom of God".

CHAPTER 10

After this, the Lord appointed seventy others, and sent them in pairs before him into all the cities and towns where he was about to go. He said to them, "The harvest is large, but the workers are few; therefore, beg the Lord of the harvest to send out workers into his harvest. Go on your way. But watch out—I send you like lambs into the midst of wolves. Do not take a wallet with you, nor a bag, nor sandals; and do not greet anyone on the

† Samaria lay on the way south to Judea and Jerusalem from Galilee. The Samaritans had a frosty relationship with the Jews.

road. And when you enter a house, first say, 'Peace be on this house'; and if a son of peace is already there, your peace will rest on him; but if not, your word will return to you unused. Remain in his house, eating and drinking what they provide, for the worker deserves his wage. Do not go about from house to house.

"And when you go into a city and they welcome you, eat what they set before you, and heal the sick there and tell them, 'The kingdom of God is near you'. But if you enter a city and they do not welcome you, go out into its streets and say, 'We even wipe off the dust that clings to our feet from your city! But know this: the kingdom of God is near.' I say to you that it will be more tolerable for Sodom on the day of judgement than for that city.

"Woe to you Chorazin; woe to you Bethsaida! For if the powerful deeds that have happened in you had taken place in Tyre and Sidon long ago, they would have repented in sackcloth and ashes. But it will be more tolerable for Tyre and Sidon in the judgement than for you. And you, Capernaum, will you be lifted up to the heavens? No, you will go down to hell.

"The one who listens to you, listens to me; and the one who despises you, despises me. But the one who despises me, despises the One who sent me."

The seventy returned joyfully, saying, "Lord, even the demons submitted to us in your name!"

And he said to them, "I have watched Satan fall, like lightning from the sky. See, I have given you authority to trample over snakes and scorpions and every power of the enemy, and absolutely nothing will harm you. But rejoice not so much that the spirits submit to you, but that your names have been written in heaven."

At that very time†, he rejoiced in the Holy Spirit and said,

....

† Literally, *in that same hour.*

"I thank you, Father, Lord of heaven and earth, because you have hidden these things from the wise and intelligent, and have revealed them to children. Yes, Father, because this was how it pleased you to do it. All things have been handed over to me by my Father, and no-one knows who the Son is, except the Father; or who the Father is except the Son, and to whomever the Son decides to reveal him."

And turning to his disciples, he said to them privately, "Blessed are the eyes that see what you see. For I tell you that many prophets and kings wanted to see what you see, but never did; and to hear what you hear, but never did."

Just then, a certain religious lawyer stood up, wanting to test Jesus. "Teacher", he said, "What must I do so that I will inherit eternal life?"

And he said to him, "What is written in the Law? How do you read it?"

The lawyer replied, "Love the Lord your God with all your heart and with all your soul and with all your strength and with all your mind; and love your neighbour as yourself".

Jesus said to him, "You have answered correctly. Do this, and you will live."

But the lawyer wanted to justify himself; so he said to Jesus, "And who is my neighbour?"

In reply, Jesus said, "A certain man was going from Jerusalem to Jericho, when he was ambushed by robbers. They stripped him and beat him and left him half-dead.

"Now by chance, a certain priest was going down that road, but when he saw the man he passed by on the other side. Like-wise, a Levite also came to the place, but seeing the man, he passed by on the other side. Then a certain Samaritan who was travelling came to the place, and when he saw the man, he was moved with compassion. He went over to him and bound his wounds, pouring oil and wine on them. Then the Samaritan lifted the wounded man onto his own animal, took him to an inn, and took care of him.

"The next day, he took out two days wages[†] and gave them to the inn-keeper, and said, 'Take care of him. And whatever more you might spend, I will pay you when I return.'

"Now which of these three, do you think, proved to be a neighbour to the man who was ambushed by robbers?"

He said, "The one who showed him mercy".

Jesus said to him, "You go and do the same".

As they were travelling, he came into a certain town. A woman named Martha welcomed him into her home, and she had a sister called Mary. Now Mary was sitting at the Lord's feet to listen to what he was saying, but Martha was worried about the many things she had to do to serve her guest. She came up and said, "Lord, don't you care that my sister is leaving me to serve on my own? Tell her to come and help me."

But the Lord answered her, "Martha, Martha, you are anxious and bothered about many things, but there is only one thing that is necessary. For Mary chose the better thing, and it will not be taken away from her."

CHAPTER 11

On one occasion, while Jesus was in a certain place and had just finished praying, one of his disciples said to him, "Lord, teach us to pray, like John taught his disciples".

....

† That is, *two denarii.*

He said to them, "When you pray, say:
'Father,
may your name be made holy[†],
may your kingdom come,
give us each day our daily bread[††],
and forgive us our sins, for we ourselves forgive everyone who is indebted to us;
and do not bring us into testing[*].'"

And he said to them, "Imagine one of you has a friend, and you go to him at midnight and say, 'Friend, lend me three loaves of bread, because my friend has arrived after a journey, and I have nothing to put before him'. And the one inside says, 'Stop disturbing me. The door is already locked, and my children are with me in bed. I can't get up and give you anything.'

"I tell you, even though he will not get up and give you bread because he is your friend, yet because of your persistence, he will get up and give you as much as you need.

"And so I tell you, ask and it will be given to you; seek and you will find; knock and it will be opened to you. For everyone who asks receives, and he who seeks finds, and to him who knocks, the door will be opened. If your son asks for a fish, which of you fathers will give him a snake instead? Or if he asks for an egg, will give him a scorpion? If you, then, who are evil, know how to give good gifts to your children, how much more will the Father give from heaven the Holy Spirit to those who ask him?"

Now he was driving out a demon that was mute. And as the demon came out, the man who had been mute spoke, and the crowds were astonished. But some of them said, "It is by

---

†   Traditionally, *hallowed by your name*.
†† Literally, *give us each day our bread for tomorrow*.
*   Or *temptation*.

Beelzebul, the prince of demons, that he drives out the demons". Others, wanting to test him, kept asking him to perform a sign from heaven.

But Jesus knew their thoughts, and said to them, "Every kingdom that is divided against itself comes to ruin; and every house against a house falls. If Satan also is divided against himself, how will his kingdom stand? For you say, 'By Beelzebul he drives out the demons', but if I drive out the demons by Beelzebul, by whom do your sons drive them out? On account of this, they will be your judges.

"However, if it is by the finger of God that I drive out the demons, then surely the kingdom of God has overtaken you. When a strong, fully-armed man guards his own house, his possessions are secure. But when a stronger man comes along and defeats him, he takes from him all the armour in which he trusted, and divides up the spoils.

"He who is not with me is against me, and he who does not gather with me, scatters. Whenever an unclean spirit comes out of a person, it passes through dry places seeking rest, and does not find any. Then it says, 'I will return to the house I came out of'. And coming back, it finds it all swept clean and in order. Then it goes and gets seven other spirits more evil than itself, and goes in to live there. And that person ends up worse off than he was at the beginning."

Now while he was saying these things, a woman from the crowd called out, "Blessed is the womb which bore you, and the breasts which nursed you".

But Jesus said, "Blessed rather are those who hear the message of God, and keep it".

With the crowds increasing around him, he began to speak: "This generation is an evil generation. It seeks a sign; but no sign will be given to it except the sign of Jonah. For just as Jonah was a sign to the Ninevites, so also the Son of Man will be to this generation. The Queen of Sheba will rise up at the judgement with the men of this generation and condemn them, because she came from the ends of the earth to hear the wisdom of Solomon. Yet something greater than Solomon is here. The men of Nineveh will rise in the judgement with this generation, and condemn it, because they repented at the preaching of Jonah. Yet something greater than Jonah is here.

"No-one lights a lamp only to put it in a cellar; instead, it is put on the lampstand, so that those who enter may see its light. The lamp of the body is your eye. When your eye is healthy[†] to others, your whole body is full of light; but when your eye is evil[††], then your body is dark. See to it, then, that the light within you is not darkness. If, therefore, your whole body is full of light, with no part dark, it will be as full of light as when the lamp shines out brilliantly upon you."

While he was speaking, a Pharisee invited Jesus to have dinner with him; and Jesus went into the Pharisee's house and reclined at the table. When the Pharisee saw this, he was astonished, because Jesus did not first ritually wash himself before dinner. The Lord said to him, "Now you Pharisees cleanse the outside of the cup and the plate, but on the inside you are full of greed and wickedness. O you fools—did not he who made the outside make the inside as well? Instead, give the contents of the cup and plate to the poor, and you will find that all things are clean for you.

----

†   The Greek word here also means *generous.*
††   To have an *evil eye* was a Jewish way of saying *miserly* or *stingy.*

"But woe to you Pharisees, because you give a tenth of your mint and rue and all your herbs, but you overlook justice and the love of God. You should have done these things, without neglecting the others.

"Woe to you Pharisees, because you love the best seat in the synagogues, and the way people greet you in the market place. Woe to you, because you are like an unmarked grave which those walking above do not realise is there."

One of the religious lawyers answered him, "Teacher, you insult us as well by saying these things".

But Jesus said, "Woe to you religious lawyers as well! For you load people up with burdens that are hard to carry, but you yourselves will not lift one finger to bear the load. Woe to you, because you build the tombs of the prophets, but your fathers were the ones who killed them! Therefore, you are witnesses and accessories to the deeds of your fathers, because they killed the prophets and you yourselves build their tombs. It is for this reason that the Wisdom of God said, 'I will send them prophets and apostles; and they will kill and persecute some of them', so that this generation might be blamed for the blood of all the prophets that has been shed since the foundation of the world—from the blood of Abel through to the blood of Zechariah, who died between the altar and the sanctuary. Yes, I tell you it will be blamed on this generation!

"Woe to you religious lawyers, because you hold the key to knowledge; you yourselves will not go inside, and you get in the way of those who do want to go in."

And as he left there, the Scribes and Pharisees began to be very resentful, and to attack him with all kinds of questions, hoping all the time to catch him out in something he might say.

CHAPTER 12

Meanwhile, a crowd of many thousands had gathered so that the people were actually trampling on one another.

Jesus began to speak first to his disciples: "Beware of the 'yeast' of the Pharisees, by which I mean their hypocrisy. There is nothing which has been concealed that will not in the future be revealed, and nothing secret that will not be made known. So, whatever you have said in the dark will be heard in the light, and what you have whispered in the privacy of your home will be proclaimed from the housetops.

"To you my friends I say, do not fear those who kill the body and afterwards can do nothing more. Let me warn you about whom you should fear: fear him who, after the killing, has authority to cast into hell. Yes, I tell you, fear him!

"Are not five sparrows sold for just a small amount[†]? Yet not one of them is forgotten in God's sight. But even the hairs on your head have all been counted. Do not fear; you are worth more than many sparrows.

"And I tell you, everyone who acknowledges me before other people, the Son of Man will acknowledge before the angels of God. But the person who disowns me before other people will be disowned before the angels of God. And everyone who speaks a word against the Son of Man will be forgiven for it; but the one who insults[††] the Holy Spirit will not be forgiven.

"Now, when they bring you before the synagogues, the leaders and the authorities, do not be anxious about how or by what you will defend yourselves, or what you will say. For the Holy Spirit will instruct you in that moment about the things you should say."

[†] Literally, *two assaria.*
[††] Traditionally, *blasphemes.*

Then someone out of the crowd said to him, "Teacher, tell my brother to divide the family inheritance with me."

But Jesus said to him, "Sir, who appointed me as judge or arbiter for both of you". And he said to the crowd, "Watch out and be on your guard against every type of greed, because one's life does not consist in the abundance of possessions."

And then he told them a parable: "The land of a certain wealthy man produced a good harvest, and he thought to himself, 'What will I do, since I have nowhere to store my crops?' Then he said, 'This is what I will do. I will knock down my existing barns and build bigger ones, and there I will store all my grain and goods. And I will say to my soul, "Soul, you have many good things laid up for many years to come. Relax; eat, drink and celebrate."'

"But God said to him, 'You fool! This very night your soul is demanded back from you. And the things you have prepared—whose will they be then?'

"This is how it will be with those who store up things for themselves, but are not rich towards God."

Then he said to the disciples, "Therefore I tell you, do not be anxious about your life—what you will eat; nor about your body—what you will wear. For your life is more than food, and your body is more than clothing. Think of the crows and how they do not sow or harvest; nor do they have a storehouse or a barn, and yet God provides for them. How much more valuable you are than the birds! And which of you by your anxiety can add a single moment to your life span? So if you cannot achieve such a small thing, why are you anxious about the rest? Think about how the lilies grow. They do not work or make clothes. But I tell you, not even King Solomon in all his glory was dressed like one of these. Now if this is the way God clothes the grass in the field, which grows today and is thrown into the incinerator tomorrow, how much more will he clothe you—people of little faith!

"And do not strive† after what you will eat and drink, or be worried. For these are the things all the nations of the world strive after, and your Father knows that you need them. Instead, strive for his kingdom, and these other things will be given to you as well. Do not fear, little flock, for it is your Father's pleasure to give you the kingdom.

"Sell your possessions and give to the poor. Make for yourselves money bags that will not wear out; a never-ending treasure in heaven, where no thief comes close, and no moth destroys. For where your 'treasure' is, that's where your heart will be also.

"Be dressed ready for work and have your lamps lit; be like people who are expecting their master to return from a banquet, so that when he comes and knocks on the door they open it immediately.

"Blessed are those servants whom the master finds alert when he returns. Truly I tell you, he will dress himself ready to work, have them recline at the table and wait on them! Blessed are those servants, if he comes at midnight or four in the morning and finds them alert.

"Now understand this: if the householder had known what time the thief would come, he would not have let him break into the house. You also be ready, because the Son of Man is coming at a time you would not imagine."

Peter said, "Lord, are you saying this parable for us or for everyone?"

The Lord replied, "Who, then, is the faithful and wise manager whom the master will appoint over his staff to give them a

† Or *seek*; also below.

food allowance at the proper time? Blessed is that servant whom the master finds doing this task when he comes. Truly I say to you, he will appoint that one over all his possessions. But if that servant says in his heart, 'My master is delayed in coming', and so begins to beat the other servants and maids, and to eat and drink and get drunk, then that servant's master will arrive on a day he does not expect, and at an hour he does not know. The master will cut him in half and assign him a place with the unfaithful.

"That servant who knows his master's wishes and does not prepare for or perform his wishes, will receive a great beating. But the one who does not know his wishes and yet does what is worthy of punishment will receive a light beating. From everyone who has been given much, much will be expected. And from the one who has been entrusted with much, even more will be asked.

I have come to bring a fire upon the earth, and how I wish it were burning already. I have a baptism to experience and how distressed I am until it is achieved. Do you suppose that I have come to establish peace in the world? No, I tell you, but rather division! From now on, five people in one home will be divided: three against two, and two against three; they will be divided, father against son, and son against father, mother against daughter, and daughter against mother, mother-in-law against her daughter-in-law, and daughter-in-law against mother-in-law."

Now he also said to the crowds, "When you see a cloud rising in the west, immediately you say, 'A rainstorm is coming', and so it does. And when a south wind blows you say, 'A heat-wave will come', and so it does. You hypocrites! You know how to interpret the appearance of the earth and sky, but why don't you know how to interpret the current time. Why also do you not judge for yourselves what is right? So as you are going with your opponent to the ruler, make an effort to settle things with him, so that he will not drag you off to the judge, and the judge hand you over to the guard, and the guard throw you into prison. I say to you, you will certainly not get out from there until you have repaid the very last coin!"

CHAPTER 13

Some of those present at that time told Jesus about the people from Galilee whose blood Pilate[†] had mixed with their sacrifices. Jesus responded, "Do you think that these Galileans were worse sinners than all the other Galileans just because they suffered these things? No, I tell you, but if you do not repent, similarly you will all perish. Or those eighteen people upon whom the tower in Siloam fell and killed them—do you think that they were more guilty than all the other people living in Jerusalem? No, I tell you, but if you do not repent, likewise you will all perish."

Then he told this parable: "A man had a figtree planted in his vineyard; he came to it looking for fruit but found none. Then he said to the gardener, 'Look, I have come looking for fruit on this figtree for three years, yet I find none. Cut it down. Why should it even waste the soil?' But the gardener answered, 'Lord, please leave it also for one more year, until I can dig around it and fertilise it. It may yet produce fruit; but if it does not, by all means, you can cut it down.'"

Now Jesus was teaching in one of the synagogues on the Sabbath Day. There was a woman present who suffered from a spirit of illness for eighteen years; she was doubled over and was unable to stand up straight. When Jesus saw her, he called her over and said, "Dear woman, be released from your illness." He laid his hands on her and immediately she straightened up and began

†   That is, Pontius Pilate, the Roman Governor of Judea.

glorifying God. But the synagogue-leader was annoyed that Jesus had healed on the Sabbath Day, and responded by saying to the crowd, "There are six days in which work should be done, so come and be healed on one of those days, not on the Sabbath Day!"

But the Lord replied, "You hypocrites! Don't each of you on the Sabbath release your ox or donkey from the feeding trough and lead it away for a drink? This woman is a daughter of Abraham. She has been imprisoned by Satan for eighteen years. Should she not be released from this prison on the Sabbath Day?"

In saying these things, those who opposed him were humiliated, yet the entire crowd was overjoyed because of the wonderful things he was doing.

So he said, "What is God's Kingdom like and to what could I compare it? It is like a mustard seed that someone took and threw into his garden. It grew and became a tree and the birds of the air nested in its branches." Again he said, "To what could I compare God's Kingdom? It is like yeast that a woman took and mixed into three cups of flour until the whole batch of dough was leavened."

Jesus was travelling through various cities and towns, teaching in them, as he continued his journey toward Jerusalem.

Someone asked him, "Lord, will only a small number of people be rescued?" And he replied to them, "Strive to enter the narrow door. For, I tell you, once the house owner gets up and locks the door, many will attempt to enter and will not be able. You may all stand outside and begin to knock on the door, saying, 'Lord, open up for us!' But he will say in reply, 'I do not remember you people or where you're from'. Then you will begin to say, 'We ate and drank with you and you taught in our streets'. But he will say to you, 'I do not remember where you come from. Get away from me, you who have committed injustices!' In that place there will be weeping and grinding of teeth, when you see

Abraham and Isaac and Jacob and all the prophets inside the kingdom of God, but you people thrown out of it. Yet, people from east and west, from north and south, will come and recline at the dining table in the kingdom of God. Indeed, some who are now last will be first, and some who are now first will be last."

At that very time, some Pharisees came to Jesus saying, "Depart from here and move on, because King Herod is looking to kill you". He replied, "Go tell that fox, 'Listen, I will continue to cast out demons and perform healings today and tomorrow, and on the third day I will be brought to my goal. But I must keep moving on today and tomorrow and the next day, because it is unthinkable that a prophet would be killed outside of Jerusalem. Jerusalem, Jerusalem, the city which kills the prophets and stones those sent to her! How often I have wanted to gather your children as a hen gathers her own chicks under her wing, yet you were not willing. Look, your house is left abandoned. I tell you, you will not see me until the time comes when you declare, 'Blessed is the one who comes in the name of the Lord'."

CHAPTER 14

One Sabbath Day, Jesus was going to the home of a leading Pharisee to eat a meal, and they were watching him. Right then a man came to him who was suffering from dropsy†. Jesus asked the religious lawyers and the Pharisees, "Is it proper to heal on the Sabbath, or not?" But they kept silent. So Jesus took hold of the man, healed him, and helped him on his way. Then he said to them, "If your son or your ox fell into a pit on the Sabbath, who among you would not pull him out straight away?" And they

---

† A medical condition characterized by an excess of watery fluid causing swelling; the modern term is 'oedema'.

were not able to give a reply to this.

When he arrived, he noticed how they all chose to sit at the places of honour. So he told a parable to the guests: "When you are invited by someone to a banquet, do not recline at the places of honour in case someone more esteemed than you has been invited by the host. The one who invited you both may come and say to you, 'Give this person your place'. And then in disgrace you will move to the last place. But when you are invited, make your way to the last place, so that when your host comes he may say to you, 'Friend, move up to a more esteemed place'. Then you will be honoured before everyone sitting at the table with you. For everyone who exalts himself will be humbled, and the one who humbles himself will be exalted."

Then Jesus said to his host, "When you put on a lunch or dinner, do not call your friends or your colleagues or your family members or wealthy neighbours, in case they return the invitation and you would be repaid. Instead, when you put on a banquet, invite the poor, the disabled, the crippled and the blind. Then you will be blessed because they do not have the means to repay you. Indeed, you will be repaid at the resurrection of the righteous."

On hearing this, one of those at the table said to Jesus, "Blessed is the person who will share a meal in the kingdom of God". So Jesus said to him, "A certain man organized a large dinner and invited many guests. At the time for the dinner, he sent his servant to say to the guests, 'Come along, for the meal is already prepared'. One after another, they all began to make excuses. The first one said to him, 'I have just bought a field and I must go out to see it. Please have me excused.' Another said, 'I have just bought five yoke of oxen and I am going to inspect them. Please have me excused.' Another said, 'I have just married a girl and so am not able to attend'. The servant went back and reported these things to his master.

"The master of the home was furious and said to his servant, 'Go out quickly into the streets and lane-ways of the city and bring in the poor, the disabled, the blind and lame'.

"Then the servant said, 'Master, what you have ordered has been done, yet there is still some room'.

"The master said to the servant, 'Go out into the highways and country lanes and convince them to come in, so that my home may be filled. For I tell you, not one of those people I previously invited will have a taste of my dinner.'"

Now, great crowds of people were travelling along with Jesus. He turned around and said to them, "If anyone comes to me and does not hate his own father, mother, wife, children, brothers and sisters, and even his own life, he is not able to be my disciple. Whoever does not carry his own cross and come after me is not able to be my disciple. For who among you would plan to build a tower and not first sit down and calculate the cost; whether you have enough to complete it? Otherwise, you may lay the foundation and not be able to finish it. And everyone who sees it would begin to mock you: 'This person began to build yet is unable to finish it'. Or what king would go out to meet another king in battle, and not first sit down to consider whether he is able with ten thousand soldiers to confront the one who brings twenty thousand against him? If he is not able, then while the other is still far away he would send out representatives to ask for terms of peace. Therefore, in the same way, everyone of you who does not give up all that you have is not able to be my disciple.

"So then, salt is good; but if it becomes tasteless, how can it possibly be made salty again? It is not suitable for the soil or the compost heap; people simply throw it away. Let anyone with ears to hear, listen!"

CHAPTER 15

Now all the tax collectors and sinners were drawing close to listen to Jesus. But the Pharisees and the Scribes were grumbling and saying, "This man welcomes sinners and eats meals with them". So he told them this parable:

"What man among you, if he owned a hundred sheep and lost one of them, would not leave the ninety-nine in the desert and go after the lost one until he found it? And when he had found it, he would lay it upon his shoulders and be overjoyed. Returning home, he would call together his friends and neighbours and say to them, 'Rejoice with me because I have found my lost sheep!' I tell you, in the same way there will be more joy in heaven on account of one sinner who repents than over ninety-nine righteous people who do not need repentance.

"Or again, what woman if she owned ten silver coins and lost one of them, would not light a lamp, sweep her home, and search thoroughly until she found it? And when she found it, she would call together her girlfriends and neighbours and say, 'Rejoice with me because I have found the lost silver coin!' In the same way, I tell you, there is joy in the presence of God's angels on account of one sinner who repents."

Jesus continued: "There was a man who had two sons. The younger one said to his father, 'Father, give me my share of the inheritance'. The father then divided the estate between the two sons. Soon afterwards, the younger son collected everything together and took off to a distant land, where he squandered his inheritance on reckless living. After he had spent everything, there was a great famine in that land, and he began to be in need. So he went and hired himself out to a citizen of that land, who sent him out to his fields to feed pigs. And he was longing to feed himself with the pods that the pigs were eating; yet no-one gave him anything. Then he came to his senses and thought, 'How many of my father's employees have an abundance of food, and yet here am I dying of hunger. I'll get up and go to my father and say to him, 'I have sinned toward God[†] and before you. I am no longer worthy to be called your son. Make me like one of your employees.' So he got up and went to his father.

"He was still some distance away when his father caught sight of him. The father was deeply moved, and running to his son he embraced him and kissed him. The son said, 'Father, I have sinned toward God and before you. I am no longer worthy to be called your son.'

"But the father said to his servants, 'Quick, bring out the best robe and dress him in it; put a ring on his finger and shoes on his feet. Bring the fattened calf and kill it. Let's eat and celebrate, because this son of mine was dead but is now alive again; he was lost but is now found.' And they began to celebrate.

"Now the elder son had been in the field, and as he drew near the house he heard music and dancing. And calling one of the hired-hands, he asked what this was all about. He replied, 'Your brother has come and your father has killed the fattened calf, because he has got him back safely'. The elder son became furious and refused even to enter the house. But his father went outside and pleaded with him. He answered his father, 'Look here! I have been serving you for so many years and have never neglected your instructions. Yet you have never even given me a goat so that I may have a celebration with my friends. Now when this son of yours, who has wasted your estate on prostitutes, comes home, you kill the fattened calf for him.'

"But the father said to him, 'My child, you are always with me, and everything that is mine is yours. But we must celebrate and rejoice, because this brother of yours was dead but is now alive, and was lost but is now found.'"

† Literally, *heaven*, and below.

CHAPTER 16

Jesus also said to the disciples, "There was a certain rich man who had a manager. This manager was accused of wasting his master's resources, and so the rich man called him in and said, 'What is this that I hear about you? Give me back your management accounts, for you cannot be my manager any longer.'

"The manager said to himself, 'What am I going to do, for my master is about to take my job away from me? I am not strong enough to dig, and I am ashamed to beg. Ah, I know what I should do, so that when I have been removed from being manager, people will welcome me into their homes.'

"And he called in each of his master's debtors, one at a time. He said to the first, 'How much do you owe my master?' He replied, '100 drums of oil'. So the manager said to him, 'Take your bill, sit down quickly and make it 50.'

"Then he said to another, 'How much do you owe?' And he replied, '100 measures of wheat'. He said to him, 'Take your bill and make it 80'.

"Now the master commended the unrighteous manager because he had acted cleverly. You see, the sons of this age are cleverer than the sons of light, when it comes to dealing with their own kind. And so I tell you, make friends for yourselves with unrighteous money so that when it fails, they will welcome you into eternal dwellings.

"The one who is faithful with very little will also be faithful with much; and the one who is unrighteous with very little, will also be unrighteous with much. If then, you have not been faithful with unrighteous money, who will entrust you with true riches? And if you have not been faithful with what belongs to someone else, who will give you things of your own? No servant can serve two masters. For he will hate one and love the other;

or he will cling onto one and despise the other. You cannot serve God and Money."

The Pharisees (who loved money) were listening to all this, and mocking him.

So Jesus said to them, "You are those who justify yourselves before other people, but God knows your hearts; for things which people value highly are detestable in God's sight. The Law and the Prophets were in place until John came. Since then, the kingdom of God is being announced and everyone is reacting violently towards it; but it would be easier for heaven and earth to pass away than for the smallest stroke of the law to fall. Everyone who divorces his wife and marries another, commits adultery; and the man that marries the divorced woman also commits adultery.

"There was a certain rich man who used to wear the finest clothes and hold magnificent parties every day. A poor man named Lazarus, who was covered in sores, lay ill at his front gate. And Lazarus longed to satisfy his hunger from the scraps that fell from the rich man's table. Not only so, but the dogs used to come and lick his sores.

"Now eventually Lazarus died and was carried by the angels to the side of Abraham†. The rich man also died and was buried. And being in the place of the dead and in torment, he looked up and saw Abraham at a great distance, with Lazarus by his side.

"He screamed, 'Father Abraham, be merciful to me! Send Lazarus to dip the tip of his finger in some water to cool my tongue, for I am in agony in this fire.'

"But Abraham replied, 'My child, remember that you received your good things in your lifetime, and in the same way Lazarus received bad things. Now he is comforted here, but you

† A euphemism for being brought into God's presence (or heaven).

are in agony. And in any case, between us and you a great chasm has been established, so that those who want to go over from here to you are not able to; nor is it possible to cross over from there to us.'

"He replied, 'Then, I beg you, Father, to send Lazarus to my father's house, for I have five brothers. He could warn them so that they might not also come to this place of torment.'

"Abraham replied, 'They have Moses and the Prophets. Let them listen to them.'

"But the rich man said, 'No, Father Abraham! But if some-one were to go to them from the dead, they would repent.'

"He replied, 'If they do not listen to Moses and the Prophets, they will not be persuaded even if someone rises from the dead'."

CHAPTER 17

Jesus said to his disciples, "It is inevitable that stumbling blocks should come, but woe to the person through whom it comes. He would be better off having a mill-stone tied round his neck and being thrown into the sea than to cause one of these little ones to stumble. Watch yourselves closely. If your brother sins, rebuke him; and if he repents, forgive him. Even if he sins against you seven times in a single day, and seven times turns back to you and says, 'I repent', then you are to forgive him."

And the apostles said to the Lord, "Increase our faith!"

But the Lord said, "If you have faith even as small as a mustard seed, you can say to a mulberry tree, 'Be uprooted and planted in the sea', and it will obey you.

"Imagine you have a servant to plough the field or look after the sheep. When he comes in from the field, which of you would say to him, 'Come at once, and recline at the table'? No, you would say to him, 'Prepare my dinner and dress yourself to wait on me while I dine, and afterwards you may eat and drink'. Do you thank the servant for doing what he was commanded to do? It is the same with you. When you have done everything you have been commanded, you should say, 'We are unworthy servants; we have only done what we were supposed to'."

On the way to Jerusalem, Jesus was passing through the border region between Samaria and Galilee. As he entered one particular town, they met ten lepers, standing at a distance. The lepers called out, "Jesus, Master, be merciful to us!"

And when Jesus saw them, he replied, "Go and show yourselves to the priests". And while they were going, they were made clean.

When one of them realised that he had been healed, he came back, glorifying God in a loud voice. He fell on his face at Jesus' feet, and thanked him. And he was a Samaritan.

Jesus responded, "Weren't there ten who were made clean? Where are the other nine? Did none come back to give glory to God except this foreigner?" And he said to him, "Stand up, and go on your way. Your faith has rescued you."

Once, when he had been asked by the Pharisees when the kingdom of God was coming, he replied, "The coming of God's kingdom is something that can not be closely observed; nor will they say, 'Look it is here, or there'. For the kingdom of God is in your midst."

He said to the disciples, "Days are coming when you will long to see one of the days of the Son of Man, and you will not see it. And they will say, 'Look it is there! Look it is here!' Do not go; and do not follow them. For the Son of Man will be like flashes of lightning that light up the sky from one horizon to the other. But first he must suffer many things and be rejected by this generation. In the days of the Son of Man, it will be just as it was in the days of Noah—they were eating, drinking, marrying and giving in marriage, until the day Noah entered the ark, and the flood came and destroyed them all. A similar thing happened in the days of Lot—people were eating, drinking, buying, selling, planting and building. But on the day Lot left Sodom, fire and sulfur rained from heaven, and destroyed them all. It will be just the same on the day when the Son of Man is revealed. On that day, no-one who is on the roof should go down into his house to get his belongings; and likewise, no-one who is in the field should turn back. Remember Lot's wife. Whoever tries to preserve his life will lose it; but whoever loses it will keep it alive.

"I say to you, on that night, two men will be reclining on one couch at the table—one will be taken and the other left. Two women will be grinding grain together—one will be taken but the other left."

They answered him, "Where Lord?" And he said to them, "Where the body is, there the vultures gather".

CHAPTER 18

Then Jesus told them a parable to the effect that they should always pray and not give up. He said, "In a certain city there was was a judge who had no reverence for God and no respect for other people. Now there was a widow in that city, who would come to him saying, 'Please help me get justice over my opponent'.

"For some time he was not willing to help. But later he said to himself, 'Though I do not have reverence for God nor respect for other people, yet because this widow is troubling me I will help her get justice. Otherwise, in the end, her constant approaches will wear me out.'"

Then the Lord said, "Listen to what the unjust judge says. Will not God, then, achieve justice for his chosen people, who cry out to him day and night? Does he delay in helping them? I tell you, he will achieve justice for them quickly. Yet when the Son of Man comes, will he find such faithfulness on the earth?"

To some who were self-confident, considering themselves to be righteous and having contempt for the rest, he also told this parable: "Two people went up to the temple to pray. One was a Pharisee, the other a tax collector. The Pharisee took his stand and was praying about himself, 'God, I thank you that I am not the same as the rest of humanity: swindlers, unrighteous, adulterers, or even like this tax collector. I fast two days a week; I give away a tenth of everything I earn.'

"But the tax collector stood at a distance and would not look up to heaven. Instead, he beat his chest and said, 'God, please be merciful to me, the sinner!' I tell you, this man went home with God having considered him righteous. The other man did not. For everyone who exalts himself will be humbled, but everyone who humbles himself will be exalted."

People were bringing infants to Jesus so that he might touch them. When they saw this, the disciples rebuked them. But Jesus summoned them and said, "Allow the children to come to me; do not prevent them. For the kingdom of God is for ones like this. Truly, I tell you, whoever does not accept God's kingdom like a child does, will not enter it."

A certain leader asked him, "Good teacher, what should I do to inherit eternal life?"

Jesus said to him, "Why do you speak of me as 'good'? No-one is good except God alone. You know the commandments: do not commit adultery; do not murder; do not steal; do not give false evidence; honour your father and mother."

He replied, "I have kept all these things since my youth".

When Jesus heard this, he said to him, "You still lack one thing.

Sell everything you have and give the proceeds to the poor, and you will have a treasure in heaven. And come follow me!" But when the man heard this he became distressed; for he was very rich.

When Jesus saw this about him, he said, "How difficult it is for those who have wealth to enter into God's kingdom. Indeed, it is easier for a camel to enter through the eye of a needle than for a rich person to enter God's kingdom."

Those hearing this said, "Then who is able to be rescued?"

Jesus replied, "What is humanly impossible is possible for God".

Then Peter said, "Look, we have left our homes and followed you".

And Jesus replied, "Truly, I tell you, there is no-one who has left house or wife or brothers or parents or children for the sake of God's kingdom who will not receive much much more in this present age, and eternal life in the age to come."

Then he took the twelve aside and said to them, "Look, we are going up to Jerusalem and everything written by the prophets about the Son of Man will be accomplished. For he will be handed over to people from other nations, and be ridiculed and insulted and spat upon. They will flog him then kill him, and on the third day he will be raised to life." Yet they did not comprehend any of these things; this saying remained hidden from them and they did not understand what was said.

As he approached Jericho, a certain blind man was sitting beside the road begging. When he heard the crowd going by, he asked what was happening. People explained to him that Jesus, the man from Nazareth, was passing by. Then he shouted out, "Jesus, son of King David, be merciful to me".

Those in the front of the crowd rebuked him, insisting that he be quiet. But he cried out all the more, "Son of King David, be merciful to me."

Jesus stopped and ordered the man to be brought to him. As he approached, Jesus asked him, "What do you want me to do for you?"

"Lord", he replied, "I want to see again".

Jesus said to him, "Then see again! Your faith has rescued you."

Immediately, he was able to see again. And he followed after Jesus, glorifying God. When all the people saw this they gave praise to God.

CHAPTER 19

Jesus entered Jericho and was passing through. There was a man there named Zacchaeus, a senior tax collector who was rich. He was trying to see who Jesus was, but because of the crowd was unable to, for he was a small man. He ran ahead of the crowd, and climbed up a fig tree to see him, because Jesus was about to pass through that way.

When Jesus got to that point, he looked up and said to him, "Zacchaeus, climb down quickly because I have to stay in your home today." He climbed down quickly and welcomed Jesus gladly into his home.

When everyone saw this, they complained, "He has gone to stay with a man who is a sinner".

But Zacchaeus stood up and said to the Lord, "Look, half of my belongings, Lord, I will give away to the poor. And if I have cheated anyone out of anything, I will repay four times the amount."

Then Jesus said to him, "Today rescue has come to this home, for this man too is now a son of Abraham. For the Son of Man came to seek out and rescue what was lost."

While they were still listening, Jesus went on to tell them a parable, because he was close to Jerusalem and the people were thinking that the kingdom of God was going to appear straight away. He said, "A certain nobleman went to a distant land to receive kingly authority and then return. He called ten of his servants, gave them ten coins and said to them, 'Do business with these while I am gone'.

"However, his citizens hated him and sent a delegation after him saying, 'We do not want this man to reign over us'. Yet he did receive his kingly authority, and when he returned he had those servants to whom he had given money summoned before him, so that he could find out what profit they had made in business.

"The first one came and said, 'Lord, your single coin has earned ten coins'. He said to him, 'Well done good servant; because you have been faithful with a small thing, take authority over ten of my cities'.

"The second came saying, 'Lord, your single coin has made five coins'. And to this one also he said, 'Take authority over five of my cities'.

The other one came saying, 'Look, Lord, here is the single coin I have stored away in a piece of cloth. I was afraid of you, because you are a strict man, taking what you did not deposit and reaping what you did not sow.' He replied, 'You wicked servant! By the words of your own mouth I will judge you. You knew, did you, that I was a strict man, taking what I did not deposit and reaping what I did not sow? Why then did you not give my money to a bank? At least then, on my return, I could have collected it with some interest.' And he said to those present, 'Take the coin from him and give it to the one who has ten coins'.

"They replied to him, 'Lord, he already has ten coins!'

"And he said, 'I tell you, everyone who has something will be given more; but from the one who has nothing, even what he has will be taken away. But as for those enemies of mine who did not want me to reign over them, bring them here and execute them before me."

After saying these things, Jesus kept moving on up to Jerusalem.

CHAPTER II

JESUS' CHRISTIAN NAME

As I said earlier, at its heart Christianity is a rescue drama. If the *status* of Jesus is captured in the title 'Christ', the *mission* of Jesus is contained in the word 'rescue'. Indeed, the role of Jesus as the rescuer was (like his status as the Christ) featured in the angelic messenger's original announcement to the shepherds about the significance of the newly born child: "Today a Saviour has been born to you in the town of David. He is the Lord Christ" (Luke 2:11). This sets up, right from the beginning, that the story which follows has to do with the threat of grave danger and the possibility of rescue.

This point is emphasized in the very name 'Jesus' itself. Most of our 'Christian' names have some meaning. 'John', for instance, means 'God's gift', which my wife thinks is pretty funny. Hers, 'Elizabeth', means 'God's pledge'. Christ was given the name *Jesus* precisely because it means literally 'God rescues'. It points to the fact that from start to finish, Jesus' mission was to lead God's rescue operation on behalf of the men and women of the world.

The obvious question, then, is: From what did Jesus come to rescue people? And how does he achieve it? That's what the next few chapters are about.

CHAPTER 12

CLEAR AND
FUTURE DANGER

An official 'doctrine' of Jesus' religious contemporaries was that God had set a day at the end of history when, as the Creator of the world, he would judge every man and woman for his or her treatment of him and of one another. This is the classic concept of the 'Judgement Day', a theme found not only in Judaism, Christianity and Islam, but also in quite an array of modern films and literature. And it arose directly out of the religious writings of the Jewish people (the Old Testament) hundreds of years before Christ. The Jews reasoned that just as a diligent parent disciplines a disobedient child, or a civilised society legislates against law-breakers, so God, because of his diligent care of humanity, would one day deal out his own justice. The reason he didn't punish until the end of history, so they explained, was to allow people the opportunity to seek his mercy and mend their ways.

There is a certain comfort and satisfaction in the concept of God's judgement. The thought that God sees every evil act perpetrated throughout history—Auschwitz, Kosovo, East Timor—and that he pledges to bring each one to justice, assures us that God is not a disinterested observer of the suffering of humanity. He is more like a caring parent or a just legislator. The Judgement Day, then, is not a theological scare-tactic designed to make people more religious. It is God's pledge to wounded humanity that he hears their cries for justice and will one day console them by bringing his justice to bear on every evil act.

There is a less comforting aspect of this idea, of course. God does not see only the great international acts of evil, such as those committed in Auschwitz or Dili. He also sees the evil closer to home; in our own country, in our own suburbs, and in our own families. He even sees the injustices of our own hearts. The view of the Old Testament, the view of Jesus' Jewish religious contemporaries, was that just as God's love was personal and individual, so his justice would be brought to bear on men and women personally and individually. It is quite an unnerving thought really!

I should make clear that, with one or two important qualifications, Jesus himself enthusiastically endorsed this belief in Judgement Day. In fact, in line with Jewish beliefs of the time (and deriving from the Old Testament), he went as far as saying that God had appointed him, as the Christ, to administer the judgements of that day. This is perhaps an unusual thought if you've never pondered it before, but it is one that we can't avoid if we are to understand the role of the Christ, as he explained it. So for instance, in Luke 13, Jesus responds to a question from his audience about how many people will escape the judgement of Judgement Day.

Someone asked him, "Lord, will only a small number of people be rescued?" And he replied to them, "Strive to enter the narrow door. For, I tell you, once the house owner gets up and locks the door, many will attempt to enter and will not be able. You may all stand outside and begin to knock on the door, saying, 'Lord, open up for us!' But he will say in reply, 'I do not remember you people or where you're from'. Then you will begin to say, 'We ate and drank with you and you taught in our streets'. But he will say to you, 'I do not remember where you come from. Get away from me, you who have committed injustices!' In that place there will be weeping and grinding of teeth, when you see Abraham and Isaac and Jacob and all the prophets inside the kingdom of God, but you people thrown out of it. Yet, people from east and west, from north and south, will come and recline at the dining table in the kingdom of God. Indeed, some who are now last will be first, and some who are now first will be last." (Luke 13:23-28).

Clearly, the one who "ate and drank… and taught" in their streets is Jesus himself. But he is also described in this analogy as "the house owner", that is, the one with the authority to open or shut the door of God's kingdom on the people of the world. The view that Jesus taught only about peace, love and harmony has little basis in the original documents. He regularly, and without the slightest hint of embarrassment, taught that God intended to bring his justice to bear on every immoral act—public or private—and that as the Christ he would be there acting as God's one-man judge and jury. To put it in the language of the above analogy, Jesus himself would be the one to "lock the door" on those who have "committed injustices".

Growing up I guess I had heard vaguely about 'Judgement Day', but I can't say I really thought about how it applied to me. To say the least, I was not a teenager with a very sensitive conscience. Even now, I can remember confronting one of the volunteer 'Scripture' teachers from school about this issue. These teachers were usually quite courageous elderly women who gave up their time once a week to teach a bunch of dis-interested, and sometimes antagonistic, students about the merits of Christianity. Unlike many of the Scripture teachers I had endured through high school—most of whom I dis-missed as "old and, therefore, in need of befriending God before they met him!"—this particular woman had me intrigued. She was highly intelligent, humorous, and more than able to out-do my smart-alec questions from the back row. Meeting a Christian like this was an entirely novel expe-rience for me.

Anyway, this woman had been teaching a little about God's judgement, and so after class one day I approached her saying, "What do think God thinks of me?". Rather than answering my question directly, this clever middle-aged mum responded with something like, "John, God knows everything about your life". She then left an awkward pause for me to ponder her statement. I thanked her for her comment and took off.

I had never been to church, never read the Bible, and never even considered becoming 'religious'. But this woman's words stayed with me for days. The thought that God had set a day in the future when he would judge people for what they had done, combined with the thought that God knew everything about my life—the good, the bad and sometimes quite ugly—gave me something to reflect on. Although this wasn't the reason I ended up embracing the Christian faith, it was probably the first time I conceded that perhaps Christianity applied to me.

CHAPTER 13

JESUS' BAD HABITS

Like any truth, a belief in God's judgement can, in the hands of the fanatical, easily become a cruel dogma by which the 'holier-than-thou' castigate and exclude the 'not-so-holy'. It contains the real and ugly possibility of allowing religious leaders the 'permission' to deem certain types of people beyond redemption.

This abusive use of the belief in God's judgement was rife amongst Jesus' religious contemporaries. Despite the Old Testament's clear teaching about God's mercy to the undeserving, many people were made to feel 'beyond redemption' by the religious leaders, particularly by the Pharisees—an elitist religious lobby group in first century Palestine, whom we come across regularly in the pages of Luke's biography.

There are plenty of modern examples, of course. I remember when AIDS first came to wide public attention. A number of religious leaders pronounced the syndrome a direct sign of God's judgement on the gay community. This kind of propaganda campaign was employed in a way that deemed gay people beyond redemption. Less dramatic examples also occur. I've met quite a number of people over the years who sadly will avoid church at all costs because of the judgemental attitudes they have experienced in the past from 'religious types'.

It was over this abusive use of the theme of God's judgement that Jesus had major disagreements with the religious
leaders of his day, disagreements that reveal to us the heart of
Jesus' mission as the rescuer.

Jesus' clashes with the authorities over the issue of God's
judgement tended to arise in the context of his very liberal
and frequent social contact with the 'not-so-religious' of his
day. Jesus was famous for his wining and dining with precisely
the sorts of people you'd expect to be first in line on Judgement Day! His activities even occasioned the quite serious
public slander that he was a "glutton and a drunkard, a friend
of tax-collectors and sinners" (Luke 7:34). It is rather interesting that the man who is now most recognisable as the
angelic holy man of stained-glass windows was originally
snubbed by religious types as a revelling alcoholic with
dubious companions. No doubt this description recorded by
Luke reflects only the exaggerated 'spin' of Jesus' opponents,
but it still tells us something fascinating about the social
habits of the real Jesus.

So, on the one hand, Jesus insisted that God was deeply
offended by human injustice and would one day bring
everyone to judgement. On the other hand, he displayed an
unusual preference for befriending those who had offended
God the most. And what's more, they seemed to love having
him around! This apparent inconsistency in Jesus' career left the
'holier-than-thou' types in his society confused and outraged.
But, of course, as you would expect, Jesus had his reasons.

CHAPTER 14

FRIEND OF 'SINNERS'

Jesus usually didn't bother trying to justify himself to his critics. He tended to let his actions speak for themselves. But on one occasion he did decide to stop and explain to the religious and not-so-religious alike exactly why his friendships with sinners were so important to him. The incident is introduced in Luke 15:1-2 in the following way:

> *Now all the tax collectors and sinners were drawing close to listen to Jesus. But the Pharisees and the Scribes were grumbling and saying, "This man welcomes sinners and eats meals with them".*

At first glance this does not seem like a very dramatic criticism. Our culture is quite comfortable with rocking the boat a little, especially if the boat is that of institutional religion. But in first century Palestine, a supposedly devout person like Jesus mixing with the obviously irreligious was a very big deal indeed. Religious teachers in this period went so far as to teach that if you shared a meal with a so called 'sinner' you were implicating yourself in their 'sins'. It says something interesting about the character and ambition of Jesus that he often chose to wine and dine publicly with many such people.

In responding to his critics on this occasion Jesus decides, as so often before, to employ what Luke calls a 'parable', a hypothetical story that conveys the point in a symbolic but powerful way. Actually, Jesus tells three hypotheticals this time, all of which are about a valuable possession being lost and then found. The first concerns a shepherd's lost sheep, the second a woman's lost silver coin and the third a father's distant son. This last one forms the climax of Jesus' explanation of his friendships with the not-so-religious, so let me point out some interesting details about it. Here's how it begins:

> *15:11 – Jesus continued: "There was a man who had two sons. The younger one said to his father, 'Father, give me my share of the inheritance'. The father then divided the estate between the two sons. Soon afterwards, the younger son collected everything together and took off to a distant land, where he squandered his inheritance on reckless living. After he had spent everything, there was a great famine in that land, and he began to be in need. So he went and hired himself out to a citizen of that land, who sent him out to his fields to feed pigs. And he was longing to feed himself with the pods that the pigs were eating; yet no-one gave him anything. Then he came to his senses and thought, 'How many of my father's employees have an abundance of food, and yet here am I dying of hunger. I'll get up and go to my father and say to him, 'I have sinned toward God and before you. I am no longer worthy to be called your son. Make me like one of your employees.' So he got up and went to his father.*

Clearly, the son in the story represents one of the 'sinners' Jesus had been mixing with, and the father, whom the son had rejected, represents God. This being the case, I am fascinated by the picture Jesus paints of what sin is. We often associate the word 'sin' with individual, immoral acts such as murder, theft, adultery, and so on. On this definition the majority of us, I assume, claim NOT to be sinners.

But Jesus' understanding of sin is a bit more subtle and quite a bit more unsettling. It has to do with the relationship (or lack of it) which people express toward God. By asking in advance for his share of the inheritance and then going off and spending it in a country far away from his father, the young man in the story was making a statement loud and clear: although he wanted to enjoy his father's resources, he wanted nothing to do with the father himself. The fact that the son spent the father's money on 'reckless living' is not so important. It is merely a symptom of the son's disrespect of the father. The real thing that makes the hypothetical son a picture of a sinner is his desire to live at a distance (relationally as well as geographically) from the father.

On this definition of sin, how many of us can claim NOT to be a 'sinner'? We, like the son in Jesus' story, keenly stake our claim on God's resources—life, relationships, food, money, the environment—but keep our distance from God himself, either by decision or neglect. We don't thank him, honour him, or even seek his advice on how the gifts of his world should be invested. We may not live 'recklessly' but we do live 'separately' from the Father. This is at the heart of 'sin', according to Jesus. It is the reason God is so offended. It is the criterion of his decisions on Judgement Day. And it is precisely what makes Jesus' rescue absolutely necessary.

Every self-respecting person in Jesus' audience that day— the Pharisees and sinners alike—would have agreed that the son in the hypothetical had caused a great offence to the father and so deserved nothing but rejection. So when Jesus spoke of the son's decision to return home and ask for a second chance, the religious people in the crowd were probably rubbing their hands with glee, expecting to hear a tale of fatherly anger and justice. After all, the father in the story represents God, and they were convinced that this is how God would treat the 'sinners' of the world.

But the Pharisees were in for a surprise. The father in Jesus' story does not at all act in the way they expected God to treat those who had offended him. The hypothetical continues:

> *"He was still some distance away when his father caught sight of him. The father was deeply moved, and running to his son he embraced him and kissed him. The son said, 'Father, I have sinned toward God and before you. I am no longer worthy to be called your son.'*
>
> *"But the father said to his servants, 'Quick, bring out the best robe and dress him in it; put a ring on his finger and shoes on his feet. Bring the fattened calf and kill it. Let's eat and celebrate, because this son of mine was dead but is now alive again; he was lost but is now found.' And they began to celebrate.*

The fact that the father saw his son while he was still "some distance away" implies that the father was already out looking for his boy. Filled with love, he runs, embraces his son, interrupts his well-rehearsed 'forgive-me' speech, dresses him in the finest clothes and throws a huge welcome home party for him. Themes of anger, justice and judgement—the things Jesus' religious contemporaries associated with God's treatment of sinners—are nowhere to be found in the story. According to Jesus, no matter how distant from God a person had become, God, like the hypothetical father, was not in the business of condemning people, but restoring and forgiving them.

This, of course, is the whole point of the hypothetical. Jesus is dramatically stating that his wining and dining with sinners is simply a reflection of God's own wish to befriend those who have lived at a distance from him. At one level, the Pharisess were correct: God is a God of justice. But they had failed to perceive a more basic aspect of God's personality: God has a passion for searching out those who are distant from him; for befriending those who are cold toward him; for rescuing those who deserve his judgement. As God's rescuer, Jesus embodied this passion, through his teaching as well as his social life.

CHAPTER 15

RESCUE IN ACTION

Luke's biography contains many examples of people moving from the danger of facing God's judgement to the safety of knowing Christ's rescue, all because of their encounter with Jesus. One of the more striking instances is found at the end of this section of Luke. It involves a man named Zacchaeus, a tax collector. He, like so many others in his profession, had kept his distance from God and decided to live for his own gain at the expense of others. He was indeed a sinner. Nevertheless, Jesus appears to have singled him out one day, and for Zacchaeus it marked a whole new beginning.

Jesus entered Jericho and was passing through. There was a man there named Zacchaeus, a senior tax collector who was rich. He was trying to see who Jesus was, but because of the crowd was unable to, for he was a small man. He ran ahead of the crowd, and climbed up a fig tree to see him, because Jesus was about to pass through that way.

When Jesus got to that point, he looked up and said to him, "Zacchaeus, climb down quickly because I have to stay in your home today." He climbed down quickly and welcomed Jesus gladly into his home.

When everyone saw this, they complained, "He has gone to stay with a man who is a sinner".

But Zacchaeus stood up and said to the Lord, "Look, half of my belongings, Lord, I will give away to the poor. And if I have cheated anyone out of anything, I will repay four times the amount."

Then Jesus said to him, "Today rescue has come to this home, for this man too is now a son of Abraham. For the Son of Man came to seek out and rescue what was lost."
(Luke 19:1-10)

It is not clear how Jesus happened to know about Zacchaeus' reputation in Jericho; perhaps it was just a miraculous insight on the part of Jesus, or perhaps when he entered the town he had simply asked people to point out to him who the most obvious sinners were. Whatever the case, despite the taboos I mentioned earlier about mixing with sinners, Jesus makes a point of selecting Zacchaeus out of the crowd so he could stay with him. Although Luke records that Zacchaeus "welcomed Jesus" into his home, the far more profound 'welcome' was the one Jesus gave him. Despite the fact that Zacchaeus had deliberately and offensively distanced himself from God, Jesus wanted to communicate—to the crowd as well as to Zacchaeus—that God was in the business of seeking out and rescuing people.

Zacchaeus is so overwhelmed by Jesus' acceptance of him, despite his faults, he responds by pledging some significant life changes—not only giving away half of his (considerable) possessions, but also repaying those he'd cheated four times the amount he owed them. Such is the impact Christ has on people when they feel themselves to be 'welcomed' by him. Hearing Zacchaeus' pledge, Jesus makes a terrifically reassuring statement to Zacchaeus. According to Jesus, people like him are precisely what his mission was all about. His life's work was "to seek out and rescue what was lost".

With these words the second big theme of Luke's portrait of Jesus reaches a climax: Jesus is God's rescuer, sent to save people from the judgement of God by offering them forgiveness and a restored relationship with their Maker.

For me, there is a question that emerges from all this: In terms of Jesus' earlier hypothetical about the distant son, am I securely within God's household or off in a far away land spending his resources while refusing his friendship? In other words, am I, on Jesus' definition, a sinner in need of rescue? The Zaccheaus episode, and the many others like it, remind us that what is hypothetical in Jesus' parable can become reality in people's lives: God forgives and forgets.

PART FOUR

TO DIE FOR

One of the historical quirks of Christianity is the fact that a cross became the symbol of the faith. Nowadays, we're used to seeing the cross adorning churches or being worn as jewellery, but this would have seemed bizarre to the people of the ancient world. The cross, after all, was an instrument of execution. It was the ancient equivalent to the electric chair or lethal injection. Imagine a miniature electric chair becoming a modern fashion accessory!

Ever since Peter had first declared him to be the Christ (in Luke 9:20), Jesus had insisted that suffering and death were at the very heart of his mission. For someone who was supposed to possess the authority of God to speak and act on his behalf, this must have sounded like a very strange ambition. I'm sure Peter and his colleagues tried their best to put this odd piece of Christ's teaching to the back of their minds and just focus on the excitement for as long as they could.

But the time soon arrived when the disciples could no longer ignore the fact that the radical claim of their leader to be both God's Christ and God's Rescuer was all too much for the authorities in the capital, Jerusalem. The life of Jesus was about to erupt into a story of jealousy, corruption, betrayal, torture and murder.

We pick up the story from the moment of Jesus' entry into Jerusalem, just a week before his execution. During these last few days his confrontations with his critics reach fever pitch and lead inevitably to the suffering and death he had spoken so much about. As Luke unfolds these events, it becomes perfectly clear why Jesus thought his death was crucial to his mission, and why ever since, a symbol of execution has become the most treasured emblem of the Christian faith.

LUKE'S BIOGRAPHY
Chapters 19–23

CHAPTER 19 (CONT.)

Jesus arrives at Jerusalem

As Jesus neared Bethphage and Bethany, at the place called the Mount of Olives, he sent out two of the disciples, saying, "Go into the town opposite. As you enter, you will find a colt tied up there on which no-one has ever ridden. Untie it and bring it here. If someone asks you, 'Why are you untying the colt?', say 'Because the Lord needs it'."

Those who had been sent went off and found things just as Jesus had told them. As they were untying the colt, its owners said to them, "Why are you untying the colt?" So they said, "Because the Lord needs it".

They brought the animal to Jesus, threw their cloaks over it and got Jesus to sit on it. As he rode along, others spread out their cloaks on the road. Now as he neared the place where the road descends the Mount of Olives, the whole crowd of disciples began to praise God joyfully and loudly because of all the mighty deeds they had seen. They declared, "Blessed be the king who comes in the name of the Lord! Peace in heaven and glory in the highest."

Yet some of the Pharisees in the crowd called out to Jesus, "Teacher, rebuke your disciples!"

Jesus replied, "I tell you, if they were to keep quiet, the stones would cry out."

As Jesus came near and saw the city, he wept over it. He said, "How I wish that you—you of all places—had recognized this day the things that bring peace! But now they are hidden from your eyes. For days are coming upon you when your enemies will set up a barricade against your walls. They will surround you and trap you from every side. They will destroy you and your children within your walls, and they will not leave a single stone upon another within you. And all this because you did not recognize the time of your visitation."

Then he entered the temple court and began to drive out those who were selling things there. He said to them, "In the Scriptures it is written, 'My house will be a house of prayer', but you have made it into a hideout for robbers!"

He was teaching daily in the temple court. But the Chief Priests, Scribes and leaders of the people were trying to kill him. Yet they could not find a way to do it, because all the people were hanging on his every word.

CHAPTER 20

One day, as he was teaching the people in the temple court and announcing the news, the Chief Priests and the Scribes approached him together with the Elders. They said to him, "Tell us, by what authority are you doing these things? Or who is the one who gives you this authority?"

He answered, "I will also ask you something; now you tell me: Was the baptism of John from heaven or of human origin?"

They discussed this among themselves, saying, "If we say, 'From heaven', he will say, 'Then why didn't you believe in him?' But if we say, 'of human origin', all the people will stone us because they are convinced that John was a prophet." And so they answered that they did not know where it was from.

Jesus said to them, "Nor will I tell you by what authority I am doing these things".

He began to tell the people this parable: "A man planted a

vineyard and leased it to tenants, and went away for quite some time. After a while, he sent a servant to the tenants so that they might give him his share of the vineyard's produce. But the tenants beat the servant and sent him away with nothing. Then he sent another servant, but they beat him also, treated him shamefully and sent him away with nothing. Then he sent a third one but they hurt him also, and cast him out.

"Now the master of the vineyard said, 'What will I do? I will send my beloved son; perhaps they will respect him.'

"But when the tenants saw him they reasoned with one another, 'This is the heir. Let's kill him so that the inheritance will be ours.' So they threw him out of the vineyard and killed him.

"So then, what will the master of the vineyard do to them? He will come and kill those tenants, and give the vineyard to others."

When those who were listening heard this, they exclaimed, "May it never be!"

But Jesus looked straight at them and said, "What then is the meaning of this passage of Scripture: 'A stone which the builders rejected has become the cornerstone'? Everyone who falls upon that stone will be broken to pieces, and anyone on whom it falls will be crushed."

The Scribes and Chief Priests wanted to lay their hands on him at that very moment, because they knew he had told this parable against them; but they were afraid of the people.

And they kept a close eye on him by sending spies who pretended to be good men. They did this to catch him out in his teaching, so that they could hand him over to the rule and authority of the Roman Governor. They asked him, "Teacher, we know that you speak and teach correctly; that you do not show favoritism, but instead teach the way of God truthfully. Is it proper for us Jews to pay a tax to Caesar, or not?"

Jesus saw through their trickery and said to them, "Show me a silver coin: whose image and inscription is on it?"

"Caesar's", they said.

He responded, "Well then, repay to Caesar the things that are Caesar's, and to God the things that are God's." They were not able to catch him out in his words in front of the people. They were amazed at his answer and became silent.

Some men from the faction of the Sadducees[†]—who say there is no resurrection—came to him. They asked him, "Teacher, Moses wrote for us that if a man's brother dies having a wife but no children, the man should marry his dead brother's wife and raise up children for his brother. Now then, imagine there were seven brothers. The first brother married and died without children. The second brother married her, then the third, and so on, until all seven brothers had died and left no children. Later, the woman herself died. In the time of resurrection, therefore, whose wife will the woman be, since all seven men had married her?"

Jesus said to them, "The people of this age[††] marry and are given in marriage, but those who are counted worthy of sharing in that age and in the resurrection from the dead will not marry or be given in marriage, for they can no longer die—they will be like angels. They will be God's children since they are children of the resurrection. Moses also revealed that the dead will be raised in the passage about the burning bush, where he speaks about the Lord as the God of Abraham and the God of Isaac and the God of Jacob. Now God is not the God of the dead but of the living; indeed all are alive to him."

Some of the Scribes responded, "Teacher, you have spoken

[†] The Sadducees were a fairly secular group within Judaism, drawing mainly from the ruling class.
[††] That is, this aeon, this period of time.

well". For they no longer dared to put any questions to him.

Then Jesus said to them, "How is it that they say the Christ is to be a son of King David? After all, in the book of Psalms, David himself states, 'The Lord said to my lord, "Sit at my right hand until I make your enemies a footstool for your feet".' Therefore, David calls the Christ 'lord'; so how can he also be David's son?"

In the hearing of all the people, Jesus said to the disciples, "Beware of the Scribes who like to walk about in long robes and love to be greeted by people in the markets, and to have the front seats in the synagogues and the places of honour at banquets. They devour the homes of widows and pretentiously say long public prayers. They will receive more severe judgement."

CHAPTER 21

Jesus looked up and noticed the rich dropping their gifts into the temple treasury. And he saw a poor widow drop in two small coins. He said, "Truly, I tell you, that this poor widow has given more than all of them. For they all gave from their surplus, but she, in her poverty, gave all that she had to live on."

When some were speaking about the temple, how it had been adorned with beautiful stones and offerings, he said, "These stones you are looking at—days are coming when not one stone will be left on another; they will all be torn down."

And they asked him, "Teacher, when will these things be, and what will be the sign when they are about to happen?"

He replied, "See that you are not deceived, for many will come in my name saying 'I am he' and 'The time is near'. Do not go after them. When you hear of wars and insurrections, do not panic. For these things must happen first, but the end will not follow at once."

Then he said to them, "Nation will rise against nation, and

kingdom against kingdom. There will be great earthquakes, and famines and plagues in various places, and terrors and great signs in the sky. But before all these things, they will seize you and persecute you, handing you over to the synagogues and prisons, and bringing you before kings and governors for the sake of my name. This will become a time for you to bear testimony. Make up your mind, then, not to prepare your defence beforehand; for I will give you speech and wisdom which none of your adversaries will be able to withstand or contradict. You will be betrayed by parents and brothers and relatives and friends. They will put some of you to death, and you will be hated by everyone because of my name. Yet not a hair of your head will be lost. Through your endurance, you will gain your lives.

"But when you see Jerusalem surrounded by armies, then know that her desolation is close. At that time, those in Judea must flee to the hills, and those in the city itself must get out, and those in the country must not enter it. For these are days when justice is dealt out, so that all that is written in the Scriptures might be fulfilled. Woe to those who are pregnant and to nursing mothers in those days, for there will be great distress in the land and Anger upon this people; and they will fall by the sword and be carried off captive to all the other nations, and Jerusalem will be trampled by the nations, until the times of the nations are fulfilled.

"There will signs in the sun and moon and stars; and on earth there will be great anxiety among the nations as they become perplexed at the sound and fury of the sea. People will faint from fear and foreboding of what is coming on the world; for the powers of heaven will be shaken. And then you will see the Son of Man coming in a cloud with power and great glory. When these things start to happen, stand up and lift your heads, for your redemption is near."

And he told them a parable: "Look at the fig tree, and all the trees. When they sprout leaves, you can see and know for yourselves that summer is near. In the same way, when you see these things happening, know that the kingdom of God is near. Truly, I tell you that this generation will not pass away until all has taken place. Heaven and earth will pass away, but my words will not pass away.

"Watch yourselves, so that your hearts will not be weighed down by decadence, drunkenness, and the anxieties of everyday life, and that day come upon you suddenly like a trap. For it will come upon all those who live on the face of the earth. But watch at all times, praying that you will have the strength to escape these things which are about to take place, and stand before the Son of Man."

By day, Jesus was teaching in the temple court, but at night he went out and stayed on the Mount of Olives. And all the people would rise early in the morning and come to the temple to listen to him.

CHAPTER 22

Now the festival of the Unleavened Bread, which is known as the Passover, was approaching, and the Chief Priests and the Scribes were searching for how they might do away with Jesus, for they were frightened of the people. Then Satan entered Judas (who was called Iscariot and who was one of the twelve). He went and made plans with the Chief Priests and the temple guards as to how he could hand Jesus over to them. They were delighted and arranged to give him money. He accepted this arrangement, and so began to look for a good time to hand Jesus over to them without a commotion.

Now the day of the Festival of Unleavened Bread arrived, in which the Passover lamb is to be sacrificed. So Jesus sent Peter and John out, saying, "Go and prepare the Passover meal for us so that we may eat it."

"Where would you like us to prepare it?" they said.

He replied, "As you enter the city, a man carrying a jar of water will meet you. Follow him to the house he goes into, and say to the owner of the house, 'The teacher asks you, "Where is the room in which I may eat the Passover meal with my disciples?"' And he will show you a large furnished room upstairs. Prepare things there."

So they went out and found things just the way he had said, and they made preparations for the Passover meal.

When the time came, Jesus reclined at the table with his apostles. He said to them, "I have intensely desired to eat this Passover meal with you before I suffer. For I tell you, I will not eat it again until it has reached its fulfillment in the kingdom of God."

He took a cup of wine, gave thanks for it and said, "Take this and share it among yourselves. For I tell you, from now on I will not drink of the fruit of the vine until the kingdom of God comes."

He took a loaf of bread, gave thanks for it, broke it and gave it to them saying, "This is my body which is given for you; do this in remembrance of me."

And in the same way, after eating the meal, he took the cup of wine and said, "This cup is the new covenant with my blood, which is poured out for you. But see, the hand of my betrayer is with me on the table. For the Son of Man is going just as it has been determined. Yet woe to that man by whom he is betrayed." Then they began to discuss among themselves which one of them was about to do this.

An argument arose among them as to which of them seemed

to be the greatest. So he said to them, "The kings of the other nations dominate their subjects, and those placed in authority over the subjects are called 'Benefactors'. But it is not to be so with you. Rather, the greatest among you is to become like the youngest, and the one who leads like the one who serves. For who is greater—the one who reclines at the table or the one serving the meal? It is the one who reclines at the table, is it not? Yet I myself am among you as one who serves.

"You are the ones who have stood by me during my trials. And just as my Father gave me kingly authority, I give the same to you, so that you may eat and drink at my table in my kingdom. And you will sit upon thrones judging the twelve tribes of Israel.

"Simon, Simon, listen! Satan has insisted that he sift you like wheat, but I have prayed for you that your faith might not fail. And when you have turned back, strengthen your brothers."

Peter said to Jesus, "Lord, I am prepared to go with you to prison and to death!"

But Jesus replied, "I tell you, Peter, before the rooster crows today you will have denied knowing me three times." Then he said to them, "When I sent you out without a wallet, bag or sandals, you did not lack anything did you?"

"Not a thing", they answered.

He said to them, "Now, however, whoever has a wallet, take it; likewise, a bag. Whoever does not have a sword should sell his cloak and purchase one. For I tell you, this piece of Scripture must be completed in my life: 'He is considered as one of the outlaws'. Indeed, this Scripture about me is even now coming to its completion."

Then they said, "Lord, look, here are two swords!"

"That is enough", he replied.

The Arrest, Trial and Execution of Jesus

Then Jesus left the house and made his way to the Mount of Olives, where he usually went, and the disciples followed him. When they reached the place, he said to them, "Pray that you will not succumb to the time of trial." And he withdrew about a stone's throw from them, knelt down and prayed: "Father, if you are willing, please take this cup away from me. Yet, may your will be done, not mine."

And getting up from his prayer, he returned to his disciples and found them asleep because of their grief. He asked them, "Why do you sleep? Arise and pray that you will not succumb to the time of trial."

While he was still speaking, a mob appeared and leading them was the man named Judas, one of the twelve. He approached Jesus to kiss him, but Jesus said, "Judas, are you betraying the Son of Man with a kiss?"

Seeing what was about to happen, those around him said, "Lord, should we strike with the sword?" And one of them struck the Chief Priest's servant and cut off his right ear.

But Jesus answered them, "Enough of this". And he touched his ear and healed him.

Jesus said to those who had come to arrest him, the Chief Priests and captains of the temple guard and Elders, "Have you come with swords and clubs, as if I am a criminal? I was with you daily in the temple, and you did not lay a hand on me. But this is your hour; this is the authority of darkness."

Then they seized him and led him away, and took him to the Chief Priest's house. Peter followed at a distance. A fire had been lit in the middle of the courtyard, and Peter sat down with those who were around it. A servant girl noticed him sitting in the light, and she stared at him, and said, "This one also was with him".

But Peter denied it, "Woman, I do not know him".

A short time later, someone else looked at him and said, "You are one of them as well".

But Peter said, "Sir, I am not".

An hour or so later, another one said quite emphatically, "In truth, this man was also with him; in fact, he is a Galilean."

But Peter said, "Sir, I do not know what you are talking about". And immediately, while he was still speaking, the rooster crowed. And the Lord turned and looked at Peter, and Peter remembered the Lord's prediction, how he had said to him 'Before the rooster crows today, you will deny me three times'. And Peter went outside and wept bitterly.

Now the men who were holding Jesus mocked him and beat him. They blindfolded him and asked him, "Prophesy! Who is it who struck you?" And they heaped many other insults on him.

As the day broke, the Elders of the people, the Chief Priests and the Scribes gathered together, and Jesus was led out before their council.

They inquired, "If you are the Christ, tell us so!"

But he replied, "If I were to tell you, you would not believe. And if I were to ask you a question, you would not answer. From this time on, though, the Son of Man will be seated at God's right hand of power."

They all said, "So you are the Son of God?"

But he replied, "You yourselves confirm that I am."

And they responded, "What more testimony do we need? We have heard it from his own mouth."

CHAPTER 23

Then the whole lot of them rose and brought him to Governor Pilate. They began to accuse him, "We found this man perverting our nation and discouraging people from paying taxes to Caesar, and saying that he himself is Christ, a king".

So Pilate asked him, "Are you the king of the Jews?"

Jesus answered, "Do you yourself say so[†]?"

Pilate said to the Chief Priests and the crowds, "I can find no fault with this man".

But they grew more insistent. "He is stirring up the people, teaching throughout the whole of Judea, starting in Galilee and ending up here."

When Pilate heard this, he asked whether the man was from Galilee. And when he discovered that Jesus was under Herod's jurisdiction, he sent him to Herod, who was himself in Jerusalem at that time.

Now when Herod saw Jesus he was overjoyed. He had been wanting to see Jesus for some time, because he had heard about him, and hoped to see him perform some miraculous sign. He questioned him at length, but Jesus said nothing in reply.

The Chief Priests and the Scribes stood there, vehemently accusing him. And Herod held Jesus in contempt, and with the help of his soldiers, he ridiculed him, dressed him in fancy clothes, and sent him back to Pilate. (On that day, Herod and Pilate became friends with each other; for previously there had been hostility between them.)

Pilate called together the Chief Priests, the leaders and the people, and said to them, "You brought this man to me as one who was perverting the people. I interrogated him in your presence, but found no cause for any of your accusations against him. Moreover, neither did Herod, for he sent him back to us. And indeed he was done nothing deserving of death. Therefore, I will order a flogging, and then release him."

But they cried out together, "Take him away! Release

....

† Or *you say that I am.*

Barabbas to us!" (Barabbas was in prison for an insurrection that had occurred in the city, and for murder).

Pilate wanted to release Jesus, and so he spoke to them again. But they cried out, "Crucify! Crucify him!"

A third time, Pilate said to them, "For what? Has he done anything evil? I have found no grounds for the death penalty in this man. Therefore, I will order a flogging, and then release him."

But the crowd kept demanding with loud voices that he be crucified; and their voices won the day. Pilate decided to grant their request. He released the man who had been imprisoned for insurrection and murder—as they requested—and gave Jesus up to what they wanted.

And as they led him away, they seized a man named Simon (from Cyrene) who was coming in from the country. They laid the cross on him, and made him carry it behind Jesus.

Now a great crowd of people followed him, including women who were mourning and wailing for him. Jesus turned to them and said, "Daughters of Jerusalem, do not weep over me; but weep for yourselves and for your children. For days are coming when they will say, 'Blessed are the barren women, and the wombs which have born no children, and the breasts which have fed none. At that time, they will say to the mountains, 'Fall on us' and to the hills, 'Cover us'. For if this is what they do when the tree is green, what will happen when it is withered?"

Two others who were criminals were also led with him to be executed. And when they arrived at the place called 'The Skull', they crucified him there along with the criminals—one on Jesus' right, the other on his left. And the soldiers divided his clothing by placing bets; and the people stood by watching.

The leaders even made fun of him, saying, "He rescued others, let him rescue himself if he really is God's Christ, his

Chosen One".

The soldiers also ridiculed him. Approaching him, they offered him bitter wine, and said, "If you really are the King of the Jews, rescue yourself". There was a placard above him which read: THIS IS THE KING OF THE JEWS.

One of the criminals who hung there was abusing Jesus, saying, "Aren't you supposed to be the Christ? Rescue yourself and us."

But the other criminal responded with a rebuke: "Have you no fear of God? After all, you are under the same death sentence. Yet, we are here justly; we are receiving what we deserve for our actions, but he has done nothing wrong."

Then he said, "Jesus, please remember me when you come into your kingdom."

And Jesus replied, "I tell you the truth, today you will be with me in Paradise".

By this time, it was already about midday. Darkness came over the whole land until three in the afternoon, because the sun stopped shining. The curtain of the Temple was torn down the middle. Then Jesus cried out in a loud voice, "Father, into your hands I entrust my spirit!" With these words he breathed his last breath.

When the centurion saw what happened he praised God, saying, "This was truly a righteous man". When the crowd that had gathered for this spectacle saw these things, they beat their chests and returned to their homes. But all Jesus' acquaintances and the women who had followed him from Galilee stood at a distance watching these things.

Now there was a man named Joseph who was a member of the Council. He was a good and just man and had not given his consent to their decision and action. He came from the Jewish town of Arimathea and was waiting expectantly for God's kingdom. He went to Pilate and asked for the body of Jesus. And when he had taken it down from the cross, he wrapped it in linen and placed it in a tomb cut out from rock, in which no-one had ever been laid.

It was the Day of Preparation, and the Sabbath was drawing near, but still the women who had accompanied Jesus from Galilee, followed Joseph and took note of the tomb and how Jesus' body was laid there. Returning home they prepared some burial perfumes and lotions. But on the Sabbath Day they rested according to the commandment.

CHAPTER 16

ONE LAST MEAL

Ever since Peter had first declared him to be the Christ, Jesus had been careful to explain that his mission would not involve conquering the enemies of God, but dying at the hands of the religious leaders. Now, a year and a half later, the moment had come. After a week of public debates and private conspiracies, the religious and political powers of Jerusalem were ready to bring Jesus' annoying influence to an end.

On the last Thursday night of his life, Jesus is well aware that time is running out, so he takes the opportunity over a meal to explain to his colleagues once again the critical importance of his death. But his is no ordinary meal. It is the Passover, the highpoint of the Jewish religious calendar, the feast where they recalled God's rescue of Israel out of the hands of Egyptian domination 1500 years before. But during this important feast, made up of fine Middle Eastern breads, spices, lamb and wine, Jesus drew his friends' attention to another rescue, the one he had embodied throughout his ministry and for which he was now about to die.

When the time came, Jesus reclined at the table with his apostles. He said to them, "I have intensely desired to eat this Passover meal with you before I suffer. For I tell you, I will not eat it again until it has reached its fulfillment in the kingdom of God."

He took a cup of wine, gave thanks for it and said, "Take this and share it among yourselves. For I tell you, from now on I will not drink of the fruit of the vine until the kingdom of God comes."

He took a loaf of bread, gave thanks for it, broke it and gave it to them saying, "This is my body which is given for you; do this in remembrance of me."

And in the same way, after eating the meal, he took the cup of wine and said, "This cup is the new covenant with my blood, which is poured out for you." (Luke 22:14-20)

Imagine someone passing you some food and wine and saying "these represent my body and blood". It would be difficult to enjoy the meal I should think. Though the disciples were no doubt getting used to things being a little less ordinary around their leader, Jesus' actions and words on this night must have stood out as particularly strange.

What Jesus did and said at this meal explains one very important aspect of his death. In stating "my body… given for you" as he handed out the bread, and then "my blood… poured out for you" as he passed around the wine, Jesus was making clear that the violent execution he was to experience in less than twelve hours was not for his own sake, but for the sake of others.

Christ's death did not fall into the category of the noble martyr who gives her or his life fighting for their cause. Nor was it merely the inevitable outworking of social and political forces which throughout history have often worked against heroic rebels like Christ. According to Jesus, his death was a purposeful act of self-giving for the benefit of others.

Precisely how Jesus' death served the interests of others becomes clearer as this Thursday night proceeds.

ONE LAST PRAYER

After the final meal with his friends, Jesus takes them for an evening stroll to a well known public garden about a kilometre from the heart of Jerusalem. It is perhaps 10pm, and the man who up until this moment has been on top of every situation, now seems troubled by the weight of the events that are unfolding. So much so, he withdraws from his friends, kneels on the ground, and makes one last prayer. The words of this prayer, which were obviously vocal enough to be heard by his colleagues twenty metres or so away, bring us to the heart of Jesus' understanding of his death.

Then Jesus left the house and made his way to the Mount of Olives, where he usually went, and the disciples followed him. When they reached the place, he said to them, "Pray that you will not succumb to the time of trial." And he withdrew about a stone's throw from them, knelt down and prayed: "Father, if you are willing, please take this cup away from me. Yet, may your will be done, not mine."

And getting up from his prayer, he returned to his disciples and found them asleep because of their grief. He asked them, "Why do you sleep? Arise and pray that you will not succumb to the time of trial."

While he was still speaking, a mob appeared and leading

them was the man named Judas, one of the twelve. He
approached Jesus to kiss him, but Jesus said, "Judas, are you
betraying the Son of Man with a kiss?" (Luke 22:39-48)

As far as we know, throughout his life Jesus had not once
baulked at the goal he had come to achieve. But now, in his
final hours, he appears to hesitate, even asking God if there
were some other way to fulfil the mission. The question arises:
What could cause a man of such resolve and ability suddenly
to hesitate?

The answer is contained in the words of his prayer: "please
take this cup away from me". At first reading, this sounds
strange. Had Jesus brought his wine glass with him from the
Passover meal? If so, why was he so concerned to get rid of it
now? Why would a mere 'cup' trouble the man who spoke
and acted for God Almighty?

But Jesus wasn't talking about a literal cup at all. He was
using a well known metaphor from ancient society. Many
prominent people in this period were assassinated by drinking
wine from a poisoned wine cup. Because this was such a
common occurrence, the phrase 'to drink the cup' became
synonymous with experiencing some tragedy or disaster. It is
similar to our metaphorical use of the phrase 'the bitter pill'.

In the Jewish culture in which Jesus lived, this same
metaphor was often used to describe the tragedy or disaster
that God would bring on nations and individuals as punishment for their injustices. The 'cup' became a symbol for God's
judgement. Let me quote just one example—there are
many—from the Old Testament (that is, the Jewish Scriptures). The prophet Jeremiah around 600 BC wrote:

This is what the Lord… said to me: "Take from my hand this cup filled with the wine of my anger and make all the nations to whom I send you drink it…" So I took the cup from the Lord's hand and made all the nations to whom he sent me drink it … to make them a ruin and an object of horror and scorn and cursing… the Lord Almighty says: "You must drink it!… You will not go unpunished."

(Jeremiah 25:15-29)

When Jesus prayed, "please take this cup away from me", he wasn't referring to a mere drinking implement. He was alluding to the outpouring of God's judgement that he was about to endure on the cross. But, of course, this would not be judgement for his own 'sins', but for those of others. At the meal, just an hour or so before, he had already explained that his body was to be "given for you" and his blood "poured out for you". These words in the garden, then, about drinking the 'cup' make clear exactly how the sacrifice of Jesus' body and blood would be for the sake of others: on the cross, he would absorb the punishment we deserve for having refused God's relationship while enjoying his resources; in other words, for our 'sins'. Jesus would drink the cup that should have been ours. And, thus, he would achieve our rescue.

It is impossible to overstate the importance of this concept for understanding Christianity. At the very heart of the Christian faith is not a set of religious rules to obey, or rituals to perform, or philosophies to comprehend, but the amazing news that God sent the Christ into the world to die for the sake of you and me.

CHAPTER 18

ONE LAST BREATH

Two themes have woven their way through the whole of Luke's account of Jesus. The first is Jesus' status over us as the Christ. The second is Jesus' mission for us as the Rescuer. Both themes are drawn together brilliantly in the account of Jesus' final moments.

After a sleepless night, two spurious legal trials and a series of public beatings and floggings, Jesus is led, carrying a large wooden beam, outside the city boundary to a rocky outcrop called the place of 'The Skull'. There, along with two other criminals, Jesus is stripped and nailed to a cross-like structure. A crowd, perhaps in their hundreds, gathers to witness the end of an extraordinary life:

Two others who were criminals were also led with him to be executed. And when they arrived at the place called 'The Skull', they crucified him there along with the criminals—one on Jesus' right, the other on his left. And the soldiers divided his clothing by placing bets; and the people stood by watching.

The leaders even made fun of him, saying, "He rescued others, let him rescue himself if he really is God's Christ, his Chosen One".

The soldiers also ridiculed him. Approaching him, they

offered him bitter wine, and said, "If you really are the King of the Jews, rescue yourself". There was a placard above him which read: THIS IS THE KING OF THE JEWS.

One of the criminals who hung there was abusing Jesus, saying, "Aren't you supposed to be the Christ? Rescue your- self and us."

But the other criminal responded with a rebuke: "Have you no fear of God? After all, you are under the same death sentence. Yet, we are here justly; we are receiving what we deserve for our actions, but he has done nothing wrong."

Then he said, "Jesus, please remember me when you come into your kingdom."

And Jesus replied, "I tell you the truth, today you will be with me in Paradise".

By this time, it was already about midday. Darkness came over the whole land until three in the afternoon, because the sun stopped shining. The curtain of the Temple was torn down the middle. Then Jesus cried out in a loud voice, "Father, into your hands I entrust my spirit!" With these words he breathed his last breath. (Luke 23:32-46)

There are two stark ironies running through this account. Nearly everyone there that day rejected Jesus' claim to be God's king, or Christ: the leaders who organized the death sentence, the soldiers who carried it out, and one of the crim- inals who hung next to him. They all saw Jesus hanging there naked, bleeding and dying, looking rather unkingly, and mocked him with words to the effect of, "If you're meant to be the Christ/King, do something!" But the irony is this: what everyone else rejected that day, the second criminal came to believe. Namely, that Jesus is the king of God's kingdom. His words make this clear: "Jesus, please remember me when you come into your kingdom".

In these words, the first major theme of Luke's biography reaches another climax. Men and women ought to acknowledge the authority of Jesus as the Christ.

The second irony is even more paradoxical. Everyone who yelled abuse at Jesus that day assumed that if he were the Christ he would rescue himself. The leaders sneered, "Let him rescue himself", the soldiers yelled "Rescue yourself", and the criminal added, "Rescue yourself and us". They figured that surely the person who was meant to speak and act for the Creator couldn't possibly wind up in such tragic circumstances. But they had failed to realise that this is exactly what the Christ had come to do. He had no intention of rescuing himself from the cross because his mission was precisely to rescue others by that cross. For on the cross he would drink the cup of judgement we deserve so that those who return to God would be rescued.

This point is skilfully emphasized in Luke's description of the second criminal. He refused to join in the insults. Instead, realising Jesus' authority, he pleaded with him for a place in his kingdom. No sooner had he said "please remember me", than Jesus responded with words of total acceptance: "You will be with me in Paradise". The criminal had found his rescue.

In these words, the second major theme of Luke's biography reaches a climax. Through Jesus Christ, men and women can find rescue from God's judgement.

CHAPTER 19

GOD THE RESCUER

The events of Jesus' final 24 hours not only underline the heroism of Jesus himself, but they also speak volumes about the Creator himself. The story of the Christ is really a story about the God whose work and passion he personified. As God's representative on earth, Jesus knew all along that his words and actions were glimpses for the world into God's own character. His teaching made God's voice heard; his healings displayed God's passion for our welfare; his forgiveness mirrored God's mercy; his command 'follow me' pointed ultimately to God's leadership.

But more than this—although it is only implicit in *Luke*, other New Testament texts (notably the Gospel of John) make clear that Christ not only 'represented' God, in the sense of being the one appointed to speak and act on his behalf, but he actually 'embodied' the presence of God himself. It turns out that the reason Jesus of Nazareth could hand out God's words, God's healing and God's forgiveness, was that God himself dwelt fully within him.

Christ's divinity—his embodiment of God—is, in my opinion, most profoundly and beautifully expressed in his death on the cross. There, in the bitter-sweet climax of Jesus' life, God himself makes known to the world the desperate measures he is willing to undertake in order to rescue us from the judgement we deserve. The very name 'Jesus'—which as I mentioned earlier means literally 'God rescues'—turns out to be not a vague statement about God's aloof intentions to rescue people, but a personal pledge about his own costly involvement in our rescue on the cross.

Thus, in the man who was willing to die for us, we actually discover the God who is anxious to rescue us. It is not hard, in light of this, to understand why the cross very quickly became the most recognisable symbol of the Christian faith.

JESUS HERE AND NOW

If only the biographies of Jesus' life had ended with the death of Jesus, we would have been left with one of the most moving and inspiring stories of history: a just, loving, heroic man betrayed and killed by proud, power-hungry religious leaders and politicians. It's the stuff of great movies; in fact, *Jesus Christ Superstar* ends in just this way. But no! All of our earliest sources for Jesus' life make the outrageous claim that a few days after his execution, Jesus was back from the dead.

This does one of two things to the news about Christ. It either robs it of any credibility, turning it into another quaint myth of the past such as the Santa Claus fable, or, if true, this claim injects the Jesus-story with unparalleled significance.

According to the most recent social research almost half of the **non**-church-going public already believe the resurrection of Christ to be an historical reality. If, however, you are part of the other half that is not quite sure what happened to Christ after his death, I have included some material on the reasonableness of the resurrection in the Extra Information section at the end of the book. It begins on page 221. After you've read Luke's claim for yourself, feel free to read this extra information before returning to my comments.

The more important question for those who already accept the resurrection as historically true is: What is the significance of Jesus' resurrection? As you read the final chapter of Luke, try to keep this question at the front of your mind.

Luke's Biography

Chapter 24

CHAPTER 24

The Resurrection and Appearances of Jesus

Now, very early on Sunday morning, the women went to the tomb with the burial lotions they had prepared. They found the stone-door rolled away from the tomb, but when they went in they did not find the body of the Lord Jesus. And as they stood there perplexed about this, suddenly two men in gleaming clothes approached them. Terrified, the women bowed down with their faces to the ground, and the men said to them, "Why do you search among the dead for someone who is alive? He is not here; rather he has been raised! Remember how he told you while he was still in Galilee, 'The Son of Man must be betrayed into the hands of sinful people and be crucified, and on the third day be raised up'." And they remembered his words.

Returning from the tomb, the women told all these things to the eleven apostles and all the other people there. (The women were Mary Magdalene, Joanna, Mary the mother of James, and some others with them.) Yet the apostles did not believe them because these reports seemed like nonsense to them.

All the same, Peter got up and ran to the tomb. Bending over, he saw the burial clothes lying by themselves. He returned home amazed at what had happened.

Now that same day, two of them were travelling to a town about eleven kilometres† from Jerusalem, called Emmaus. They

† Literally, *sixty stadia.*

were talking with each other about all that had happened. While they were talking and discussing, Jesus himself approached them and began to walk alongside them, but their eyes were kept from recognising him.

He asked them, "What are these things you are discussing with each other as you walk along?" They stood there depressed, and one of them, whose name was Cleopas, asked, "Are you the only visitor to Jerusalem who does not know about the events that have taken place there in these days?"

"What events?" he asked.

They replied, "The events surrounding Jesus of Nazareth, who was a prophet powerful in word and deed before God and all the people, and how the Chief Priests and our leaders handed him over to a death sentence and crucified him. We were hoping that he was the one who was going to redeem Israel. But on top of all this, it is now the third day since all these things happened. And then to add to it, some women from our group surprised us. They were at the tomb early this morning, and when they didn't find the body they came saying that they had seen a vision of angels, who said he was alive. And some of those with us went back to the tomb and found it exactly as the women described, but they did not see him."

And Jesus said to them, "You are so foolish and slow of heart to believe all the things the Prophets foretold! Didn't the Christ have to suffer these things and so enter his glory?" And beginning with the writings of Moses and all the prophets, he explained to them the things written about himself in all the Scriptures.

They approached the town where they were going and Jesus gave the impression he was going further on. But they urged him, "Stay with us because it is evening; the day is already over."

So he went in to stay with them. When he was reclining at

the table with them, he took the loaf of broad, gave thanks, broke it and gave it to them. Then their eyes were opened and they recognized him, but he disappeared from their sight. They said to one another, "Were not our hearts on fire as he spoke to us on the road and explained the Scriptures to us?"

They got up straight away and returned to Jerusalem, where they found the eleven apostles and those with them gathered together, who said, "The Lord really has been raised to life, and he has appeared to Simon." Then the two related the things that had happened on the road, and how they had recognized him when he broke the loaf of bread.

While they were talking about these things, Jesus stood right in the middle of them and said, "Peace to you". Thinking they were seeing a spirit, they were startled and terrified.

But Jesus said to them, "Why are you disturbed and why do doubts arise in your hearts? Look at my hands and feet, for it really is me. Touch me and see, for a spirit does not have flesh and bones, as you can see I have." He said this, and showed them his hands and feet. But when they still did not believe because of joy and amazement, he said to them, "Do you have anything here I can eat?" So they handed him a piece of cooked fish. He took it and ate it right in front of them.

Then he said to them, "I told you about these things while I was still with you: everything that is written about me in the Law of Moses, the Prophets and the Psalms had to be fulfilled". Then he opened their minds to understand the Scriptures and said, "This is what is written: the Christ will suffer and rise from the dead on the third day, and in his name repentance for the forgiveness of sins will be announced to all nations, beginning from Jerusalem.

"You are witnesses of these things, and so I will send to you the promise of my Father. You yourselves stay here in the city until you are clothed with power from heaven."

Then he led them out to Bethany. He raised his hands and blessed them. As he was blessing them, he departed from them and was taken up into heaven. They worshipped him and then returned to Jerusalem with great joy, where they were always in the temple court, praising God.

CHAPTER 20

DEAD MAN WALKING?

Ever since Peter had first confessed his belief that Jesus was the Christ, Jesus had tried to explain to his colleagues that not only would he suffer and die, but he would be raised to life again a few days later. You may remember Jesus' words:

> *The Son of Man must suffer much and be rejected by the elders and Chief Priests and scribes and be killed and, on the third day, be raised up. (Luke 9:22)*

It is difficult to know what the disciples would have made of these words. Apart from the doctrine about the dead coming back to life on the Day of Judgement, the notion of someone rising from the dead was not really part of Jewish beliefs. The disciples must have placed Jesus' talk of resurrection, like that of his death, in the theological too-hard-basket. They undoubtedly would have expected him to rise with everyone else on Judgement Day; but the fact that some disciples went to the tomb on Sunday morning intending to embalm the dead body, certainly suggests they had no expectation that Jesus was about to rise to life then and there.

The accounts that follow the women's discovery of the empty tomb make clear that the resurrection Jesus had spoken of to his disciples was not a near-death-experience or a mere revival of a corpse. It was an event of a very different kind.

The first appearance of the resurrected Jesus is rather confusing at first. He conceals himself from two rather depressed disciples making their way (probably home) to a town called Emmaus, 11 kilometres from Jerusalem (where Jesus had been killed a couple of days before). Luke reports that "Jesus himself approached them and began to walk alongside them, but their eyes were kept from recognizing him". Then, after a lengthy discussion about the events of the past week, they suddenly recognized him. But as soon as they did he "disappeared from their sight".

Turning around, these men race straight back to Jerusalem to tell the others what they had seen. Luke then recounts:

While they were talking about these things, Jesus stood right in the middle of them and said, "Peace to you." Thinking they were seeing a spirit, they were startled and terrified.

Again, Jesus' sudden appearance in the middle of a crowed room suggests that there is something different about Jesus' existence after his resurrection. He certainly didn't go around appearing and disappearing before his death. Even those closest to him thought they were seeing a 'spirit' or a ghost. Something has happened to Jesus' 'body'. This is not merely the revival of his corpse.

Some modern writers have looked at these unusual aspects of the reports about Jesus' resurrection and mistakenly concluded that what we are dealing with here is not a concrete, bodily 'resurrection' at all, but merely a ghostly, 'visionary' experience on the part of the bewildered and depressed disciples.

But this is to miss the point entirely. Luke (and all the

other biographers as well) make perfectly clear that despite the unusual 'properties' of Jesus' body after the resurrection, it is still a physical body. This is explicit in Jesus' words to the startled disciples:

> *But Jesus said to them, "Why are you disturbed and why do doubts arise in your hearts? Look at my hands and feet, for it really is me. Touch me and see, for a spirit does not have flesh and bones, as you can see I have." He said this, and showed them his hands and feet. But when they still did not believe because of joy and amazement, he said to them, "Do you have anything here I can eat?" So they handed him a piece of cooked fish. He took it and ate it right in front of them. (Luke 24:36f)*

So, on the one hand, Jesus' resurrected body appears to be perfectly natural (eating, bearing scars, and so on), but on the other, it seems to have undergone a radical change (appearing, disappearing, and so on). What accounts for this strange situation? The answer is found in the fact that Jesus' resurrection is not to be understood as a mere resuscitation. It was, according to him, an 'exaltation'.

CHAPTER 21

GOD'S RIGHT-HAND MAN

In his resurrection, Jesus was not simply *returned* to his former glory, he was *elevated* to a new kind of glory. In fact, 'glory' is precisely what Jesus called it. Just before he disappeared from the sight of the two men travelling home from Jerusalem to Emmaus, Jesus explained something of his resurrection to them:

> And he said to them, *"You are so foolish and slow of heart to believe all the things the Prophets foretold! Didn't the Christ have to suffer these things and so to **enter his glory?"**
> (Luke 24:25)

We often associate the word 'glory' with victory or success, particularly in sport. Those collecting gold medals at the Olympic games are often described as achieving 'Olympic glory'. The winner of the Rugby World Cup achieves 'Rugby glory', and so on.

So what is Jesus' 'glory' all about? Put simply, Jesus understood his resurrection to be his entrance into a leadership on God's behalf that would last forever. The Old Testament prophets I spoke about earlier all promised that the coming Christ would rule, not temporarily, but eternally (for a discussion of the many prophecies in the Old Testament con-

PART FIVE: JESUS HERE AND NOW

cerning the Christ, see the Extra Information section starting at p.211). It is difficult to imagine how ancient Jews interpreted these prophecies, since they, like us, knew very well that human beings—even kings—tend to die eventually. When Jesus travelled around Palestine for three years, teaching, healing, forgiving and calling people to follow him, this was only ever going to be local and short-lived; a kind of advanced screening of the major feature. After his death and burial, however, God raised Jesus to a real, but totally new, existence that would be eternal and universal, not just temporary and local. All the power, wisdom, authority, forgiveness and leadership that Jesus had demonstrated during his three year public career, would now become eternal realities. Jesus was exalted; he had entered his 'glory'.

Jesus had spoken of this eternal rule or glory, though in different words, a few days earlier at his court trial before a full council of the civil and religious leaders of Jerusalem.

> *As the day broke, the Elders of the people, the Chief Priests and the Scribes gathered together, and Jesus was led out before their council.*
>
> *They inquired, "If you are the Christ, tell us so!"*
>
> *But he replied, "If I were to tell you, you would not believe. And if I were to ask you a question, you would not answer. From this time on, though, the Son of Man will be seated at God's right hand of power."*
>
> *They all said, "So you are the Son of God?"*
>
> *But he replied, "You yourselves confirm that I am."*
>
> *And they responded, "What more testimony do we need? We have heard it from his own mouth." (Luke 22:66-71)*

If Jesus had been at all interested in avoiding the ugly fate that awaited him, now was his last chance. He could easily have softened his description of himself, claiming merely to be a humble, misunderstood Jewish teacher. Instead, Jesus makes one of the most bald and bold statements yet: "From this time on, though, the Son of Man will be seated at God's right hand of power".

In the minds of his enemies, this trial and execution would mark the end of Jesus' great influence over the people of Palestine. But for Jesus, it marked simply the end of the preview and—with his resurrection—the beginning of the main feature. He claimed that from this point on he would be exalted to a throne at "God's right hand of power", a striking metaphor of his eternal rule on God's behalf. To use our modern equivalent, Jesus was to be God's 'right-hand-man'. The religious leaders, of course, understood precisely what Jesus was saying and immediately sought to seal his fate.

Christ's resurrection was not merely the Creator's way of thumbing his nose at Jesus' religious enemies: "Ha, you may have killed him, but I revived him!" Put simply, the resurrection was God's elevation of his Christ from a position of local, temporary authority within Israel to one of permanent authority over the whole world. It was the ultimate 'glory'!

CHAPTER 22

JESUS HERE AND NOW

If Jesus has been raised from death, to be "seated at God's right hand of power", it means that the news about Christ is not just a fascinating story from the past, but an important reality for the present. And so it is crucial to begin unpacking what all this means today.

This book began with the definition that Christianity was simply, 'responding appropriately to the news about Jesus Christ'. In light of the whole story of Christ, from birth to resurrection, what then is the 'appropriate response'? Fortunately, we don't have to speculate about this because Jesus himself answered that question shortly after his resurrection.

On the occasion when Jesus appeared to the group of his followers and ate some fish before them, he explained with crystal clarity what they were to announce to the world in light of his life, death and resurrection. It is the announcement Christianity has made to men and women ever since.

Then he said to them, "I told you about these things while I was still with you: everything that is written about me in the Law of Moses, the Prophets and the Psalms had to be fulfilled." Then he opened their minds to understand the Scriptures and said, "This is what is written: the Christ *will suffer and rise from the dead on the third day, and in his name **repentance for the forgiveness of sins** will be announced to all nations, beginning from Jerusalem."* *(Luke 24:44-47)*

According to Jesus, the events of his life create both a demand and an offer. The demand is described as 'repentance' and the offer as 'forgiveness of sins'. Since these two ideas summarize the appropriate response to Christ, let me try to unpack them a little.

CHAPTER 23

REPENTANCE:
A CHANGE OF MIND

Unfortunately, the word 'repentance' has some bad connotations these days. It conjures up images of an angry preacher, thumping his pulpit and telling us to pull our socks up and be good or else face the fires of hell. Or perhaps you, like me, have thought of it as a kind of spiritual swear-word, something nasty that religious people are allowed to say to unreligious people. What Jesus said here is quite different.

'Repentance' is a *turnaround of attitude that accepts God's agenda—about himself, Christ and ourselves—above our own.* Luke's account of Christ's life is full of examples of people repenting: think of the 'sinful woman' (in Luke 7, page 55) who gave up her own view of how life should be lived and came to Jesus for a brand new beginning; or the apostle Peter (in Luke 9, page 62) who put aside the widespread misconceptions about Jesus and acknowledged that he was in fact "the Christ of God"; or the wealthy tax collector, Zacchaeus (in Luke 19, p.123), who responded to the welcome of Jesus by publicly vowing to treat people God's way from that moment on.

Perhaps the best illustration of 'repentance' is found in Jesus hypothetical, or parable, about the distant son (in Luke 15, page 114). Having taken his father's riches and spent them on himself in a far-away land, the son decides to return home and plead for fatherly mercy. Of course, this is a picture of you and me realising that we've lived at some distance from God—enjoying his resources while refusing his involvement in our lives—and deciding to return to him.

This idea of a shift in attitude is central to the word 'repentance' itself. The Greek word we translate as 'repentance' is *metanoia*. 'Meta' means *change* and 'noia' means *mind*. Knowing this helps to dispel a common misconception about Christianity. People often understand the Christian faith as involving primarily a transformation of lifestyle—going to church, saying prayers, obeying certain ethical commands. But if Jesus had intended to emphasize these things, the word here at the end of Luke's biography would probably have been *metamorphe* (from which we get the English 'metamorphosis'), which means a 'change of form' or 'behaviour'. But Christianity is much more than a transformation of behaviour; it concerns a transformation of our whole outlook on life.

A changed outlook will, of course, lead inevitably to some changes in lifestyle, and a significant portion of Jesus' teaching in Luke chapter 6 (pages 49-52) and chapter 12 (pages 104-108), for instance, is devoted to describing some of the ways God's outlook will shape our everyday lives. But the point must never be lost: it is the changed mindset or outlook that leads to a new lifestyle, and not the other way around. Jesus was not interested in merely external obedience to religious behaviours—this, after all, is what he criticised the Pharisees for. He did not come to teach 'morals' so that I could become a 'good person' (he didn't appear to believe there was such a thing); he came to evoke 'repentance', a transformation of my mindset.

Only this constitutes the 'appropriate response' you and I are to make to the news about Christ.

The word 'repentance' brings the first major theme of Luke's biography to its final climax. If Jesus is the Christ, the one who rules on God's behalf (both then and now), the appropriate response for you and me is to change our minds about whose agenda we will live by. It makes perfect sense for the words 'follow me' to become the recurring theme of the rest of our lives.

Jesus believed that his life, death and resurrection would demand 'repentance' from people, but he knew also that these events established an extraordinary offer for humanity: "the forgiveness of sins".

CHAPTER 24

FORGIVENESS: a FRESH START

As I've said before, Christ taught that God is personally offended at the way we enthusiastically enjoy the gifts of his creation—food, wine, relationships, the environment, art, technology, sex, beauty—but work hard at keeping our distance from the Creator himself. We don't thank him, honour him, or even seek his advice on how these gifts ought to be employed. According to Christ, this is what the Bible means by the word 'sin', and God is so offended by it that he has pledged to bring every act of sin to justice on Judgement Day. Jesus even taught that, as the Christ, he would be there to officiate at this Judgement.

Nevertheless, here at the end of Luke's biography Jesus pledges that just as the returning son in his earlier parable found unconditional acceptance from the father, so anyone who 'repents' will receive God's complete forgiveness of all their sin. The offence they've caused God and the judgement due to them on Judgement Day will evaporate. God will, quite literally, forgive and forget.

There is a striking scene in the musical *Les Miserables*, in which the lead character, a roguish petty thief named Jean Valjean, is taken in for the night by a local church official, a bishop no less. The bishop feeds him, gives him a fresh set of clothes and offers him a room for the night. Over dinner Valjean notices a beautiful silver candelabra on the mantle piece. He decides to steal it during the night. While the bishop is sleeping, Valjean creeps through to the dining room, places the candelabra in his bag, and takes off into the night. Within moments he is caught red-handed by a policeman who spots him leaving the residence. He is taken straight back, the bishop is woken up, and with candelabra in hand the policeman asks, "Sir, what shall I do with this criminal?" The bishop responds, "No officer, you don't understand. This is my dear, long-time friend. The candelabra was a farewell gift, given to him just last night. In fact, I am surprised he didn't take my other gifts." Reaching to the cupboard the bishop handed a stunned Valjean various other expensive pieces of silverware.

Confused, the policeman apologized for any trouble he'd caused and departed, leaving the bishop alone with his thief. The bishop silently filled Valjean's bag with the gifts and sent him on his way, wishing him God's every blessing. Valjean is dumbfounded.

This night was to become the defining moment in Jean Valjean's life. For the rest of the musical, through song and dialogue, Valjean will refer back to the kindness of the bishop as his one encounter with 'grace'—unconditional forgiveness in the face of his great shame. For the rest of the story he is a changed man.

The events of Christ's life create a similar possibility for the world. Because of Jesus, people like you and me can experience God's transforming, unconditional forgiveness. No matter what we've done to offend God, Christ inaugurated a period of amnesty between the Creator and his creation.

The phrase 'forgiveness of sins' brings the second major

theme of Luke's biography to its final climax. As the Rescuer (both then and now), Jesus embodies God's sentiments toward those who have kept their distance from him. He wined and dined with 'sinners' to convince them that the Almighty wanted to bridge the gap between them and himself, to offer them forgiveness despite what they'd done to offend him. According to Jesus, God wanted men and women to have a life-changing encounter with his 'grace'. Of course, this is seen most clearly in the fact that Jesus' central mission in life was to die on our behalf, to take upon himself the punishment that should have been ours, so that those of us who 'repent' could experience 'the forgiveness of sins'.

Christianity is simple really. It's not a philosophical system, a code of morals, or a set of rituals. It's the news about God sending his promised Christ to speak and act on his behalf, and to die and rise for our forgiveness. In other words, it is a *yarn* that calls for a *response*—and both are summarized in Jesus' parting words to his disciples. Let me quote them once more:

> *The Christ will suffer and rise from the dead on the third day, and in his name repentance for the forgiveness of sins will be announced to all nations.*

Almost 2000 years later, in a nation on the other side of the globe, I have tried to echo Luke's announcement of this message. I hope that you can see that Luke has pushed us way beyond 'religion', with all its burdens and distractions. He has left us not with a peculiarly Anglican, Presbyterian, Roman Catholic or Baptist Christianity.

He has given us simply Christianity.

Extra Information

In the pages that follow, I have provided some extra information on different subjects that may be useful to readers of Luke's Gospel:

- If you have questions about the truth and reliability of Luke's biography, and the Bible generally, see Extra Information I;
- If you would like more information on how the Old Testament Scriptures predicted and pointed forward to the coming of Jesus Christ, read Extra Information II;
- If you would like to delve further into the arguments and counter-arguments for Jesus' resurrection, these are contained in Extra Information III;
- And if have been challenged by Luke to respond appropiately to the news about Jesus Christ, see Extra Information IV for some suggestions about where you can take it next.

GOSPEL
TRUTH OR MYTH?

It is occasionally said that the Gospels (and the Bible generally) are full of 'myths'. Actually, the longer I think and the more I read on this issue, the more I'm convinced that the real myths are those **about** the Gospels, not in them. In the next few pages, I'd like to explain why.

THE 'MYTH' OF LANGUAGE TRANSLATION

The Gospel of Luke was not written in English. I guess that goes without saying. But what language was it written in? Who on earth now understands a language that is more than 2000 years old? And how many languages has this biography been translated into before it ended up in English? Questions like these are good ones, but in popular discussion have given rise to what you might call the 'myth of language translation'. That is, the view that the Bible was written in one 'dead' language, then translated into another 'half-dead' one, which was then translated into Latin, German and eventually English, and 'ye olde' English at that. Thus, even if you could make sense of the English Bible you could never be sure that this multiple translation process had not lost a lot of the meaning of the original words.

It is certainly true that Late Antique Koine Greek, the language in which Luke's biography was written, is no longer used to order a lamb souvlaki at the local deli—not even in the most traditional Greek villages. But ancient historians and biblical scholars do read and understand it. In fact, many church ministers you'll come across know the language. Although it's a 'dead' language in terms of modern popular usage, it is very much alive in historical, literary, church and theological circles. And actually our knowledge of this language is not getting worse with time; it is getting much better. The more and more ancient Koine Greek documents that are found—and there are thousands of them—the more we can compare the meaning and usage of certain ambiguous words and, therefore, the more accurately scholars can translate the Bible.

As for the idea that there are a lot of languages in between our modern Bibles and the original ones, this is simply not true. Almost every modern English Bible on the market today is a direct translation of the ancient languages in which it was written (Hebrew and Aramaic for the Old Testament and Koine Greek for the New Testament). The translation of Luke's biography used in this book was made directly from Koine Greek.

Of course, there are some things that can't be translated: for instance, rhymes and puns are virtually impossible to convey poetically in another language. However, this is not peculiar to Bible translation, and since there is not a lot of poetry in Luke's biography we hardly need to be concerned.

THE 'MYTH' OF COPYING ERRORS

If you decided to copy out by hand the words of this particular page, chances are you'd make a mistake, perhaps two. These are not likely to be major mistakes—a misspelling here, a missed word there—but it would probably not be exactly the same as the printed page. Now suppose someone copied your page, then someone copied theirs and so on. Even if only a few mistakes were made over several copies, if this process went on for hundreds of years the differences between the final copy and the original page might be quite dramatic.

Could this not have happened to Luke's biography? After all, two thousand years is a lot of copying.

Well, the answer is 'yes' and 'no'!

The first thing to keep in mind is that the scribes responsible for the copying process didn't think they were passing on just the daily comic strip or the weekly TV guide. They thought they were reproducing 'divine words'. That is, they regarded Luke's writings as orchestrated by God himself, the same God Jesus had spoken so much about. Whether or not we moderns accept their view, the fact is, it had quite an influence on the care these scribes took in their copying task. Imagine thinking that the next letter you scribbled down was of everlasting importance and that God himself was watching over your shoulder. I'm sure you would write with extreme seriousness. So did the scribes.

The second thing to remember is that there was a 'scribal' culture in this period of history. What I mean is that copying documents by hand was a highly esteemed job in the ancient world. Some 'scribes' were full-time professionals, not just in religious communities but also in royal and political circles. We have no way of knowing how many of the Christian scribes were 'professionals', but the point is that this was a task not given to just anyone who could hold a pen in their hand. The standards were, on the whole, very high.

Nevertheless, mistakes were made. Words were misspelt or

missed out, whole lines were overlooked, and pages went missing. But in some way, I am glad this was the case. The fact that we can spot these mistakes actually underlines just how reliable our modern Bibles are. Let me explain.

Let's suppose Luke completed his biography in Antioch (Syria), made several copies and sent them off to various destinations for discussion and reflection. These would have been copied immediately, and due to the importance of the document, quickly sent off to other people and communities. Within a short space of time there would have been hundreds of copies of Luke's biography disseminating throughout the Roman Empire, in Syria, Israel, Egypt, Greece and Rome itself.

As the years passed and the number of copies increased, the mistakes —though relatively few—might begin to mount up. Now if our modern version of Luke's biography were based on just one ancient manuscript of the book, we may well have reason for suspecting that this one document had changes within it. And the problem would be that without other copies of the document we wouldn't be able to discover which sentences had mistakes in them. But fortunately we don't have this problem at all. In fact, we (I mean the major libraries of the world) have twenty ancient manuscript copies of Luke's biography (or sections of it) uncovered from all around the Mediterranean, from different periods of the copying process. This is great news because it means we can take a manuscript of Luke found, say, in Egypt, dated at 700 AD, compare it with one found in Rome, dated at 500 AD, and then compare them both with one found in Turkey, dated at 200 AD. Because there are so many of these manuscripts, the detective work of scholars is made all the easier.

Here's an example of what I mean. In the last few sentences

of Luke's biography, he writes of Jesus' farewell to his disciples:

*As he was blessing them, he departed from them, **and
was taken up into heaven.***

The words "and was carried up into heaven" are missing from
some of the ancient versions of the biography. Now if we only
possessed these few versions of Luke, this statement would
not appear in modern Bibles. However, as I said, we have
many other manuscripts, and in the great majority of them
these words do appear. What's more, they appear in the oldest
manuscript copy of Luke (dated 200 AD). This makes it very
likely that these words are original and that the scribe responsible for the omission simply overlooked them. Perhaps the
scribe was so excited to be near the end of the book he or she
jumped to the next line a little too quickly.

This is not the only 'mistake' found in ancient copies of
Luke, but the sheer number of copies we have, from different
parts of the ancient world, from varying stages of the copying
process, means that mistakes like these are easily found and
quickly ironed out in our modern Bibles. You can be confi-
dent that what we read today in Luke's Gospel is what he
penned nearly 2000 years ago.

THE 'MYTH' OF LIES AND BIAS

Even if we suppose that modern translations are accurate and
that 'mistakes' in the ancient manuscripts are easily ironed
out, this still leaves the awkward possibility that Luke and the
other biographers of Jesus were simply not telling the truth.
In broad terms, there is little doubt about the main 'plot' of
Jesus' life. As we saw earlier, even if we never had the Bible,
we would still be able to piece together the major events of

Jesus' life. But as they say, 'the devil is in the details'. Perhaps the details of Jesus' life contained in the Gospels are incorrect. Either the biographers simply lied or their biases were so strong that the facts of the matter have been obscured beyond recognition. In other words, perhaps all we have today in the Gospel of Luke is a well-preserved tale.

The suggestion that the biographies consist of straight out lies is not very compelling given the nature of the books. To begin with, keep in mind that all four biographies are based on eyewitness accounts. Mark's biography was written by an associate of the Apostle Peter, one of Christ's closest companions. What Mark wrote down was what Peter insisted took place. Luke's biography was also based on eyewitness information. In his opening paragraph, as we saw, he makes clear that he has worked hard to make sure his account relies on the best witnesses. In other words, the Gospels of Mark and Luke are analogous to you interviewing me to write an essay on my wife, Buff. That gets you pretty close to the events themselves. The other two Gospels (Matthew and John) are even closer, since they appear to have been written by eye-witnesses themselves (although in Matthew's case this is less certain): men who travelled and worked with Jesus for over three years. This would be like me writing an essay on Buff.

So why are these eyewitness accounts not simply to be disregarded as lies? The answer has to do with what we know of the fate of the eyewitnesses. Imagine you did decide to write a report of my wife's life based on my eyewitness information, and in that information there were some quite sensational revelations about Buff's deeds and talents. After some time a little controversy might develop about how much of my information were true and how much were false. If, as a result of my sensational claims about Buff's abilities, I became quite wealthy and famous, attracting great interest from other publishers and media organizations, people might begin to wonder if I had simply made up the stories to promote myself. People's suspicion about my information would be quite reasonable under these circumstances.

Suppose, however, that my claims did not promote my interests, but instead brought me nothing but ridicule and anger from the community at large. Suppose that I was arrested for public fraud and forced to retract my statements, something I refused to do all the way to my death. Although this would not prove my claims, it would make it difficult to dismiss them as straight out lies. I am sure you can see what I am getting at.

The fate of many of the main eyewitnesses of Jesus' life, upon whom the Gospels are based, headed in a similarly tragic direction. Far from being promoted in their society by their sensational claims about Jesus, they were ostracised, excommunicated, imprisoned, tortured and, in some cases, executed for their stories—Apostle James, beheaded, Jerusalem, 44 AD; Apostle Peter, executed (perhaps by crucifixion), Rome, 64 AD; James, brother of Jesus, stoned and clubbed to death, Jerusalem, 62 AD; Apostle Paul, beheaded, Rome, 65 AD.

This poses a serious historical question for anyone thinking through these issues. Why, if the story of Jesus was largely a fraud, did those who knew the 'truth' willingly suffer and die for their claims? It is one thing to die for an ideology that one simply *believes* to be true—some Muslim extremists and aberrant Christian cult members have done that in recent times— but it is another thing entirely to die for a claim which you *know* to be a lie. Luke's biography (like the others') is based on the claims of eyewitnesses who suffered and even died for their reports. This is not easy to dismiss as simple fraud.

Most people do not go as far as claiming that the biographies are based on lies. Instead, they somewhat less offensively suggest that the eyewitnesses or the biographers themselves were so impressed with Jesus that their bias overran their ability to report accurately. This is more reasonable than the suggestion that the first Christians simply lied, but it still has problems of its own.

To begin with, it is hard to see how simple bias would account for many of the events recorded in the Gospels. Bias usually just exaggerates things that are rooted in reality: the length of the fish, the size of the golf handicap, the beauty of my daughter's eyes. One can imagine, I guess, the first Christians exaggerating, for example, the number of people who followed Jesus into the desert one day—perhaps it was more like one thousand than the "five thousand" recorded in Luke 9:10-17. This is the sort of thing that bias produces. But what on earth could have produced the story of Jesus walking on water? Could it be an exaggerated version of a story about Jesus going for a swim? I doubt it. Nor can it be explained by the viscosity of the Dead Sea (as one of my slightly sceptical mates recently suggested), since even at its most solid, the Dead Sea only allows enhanced floating on your back, not walking! Besides, it was the Sea of Galilee that Jesus is reported to have walked on.

And what about the claim that Jesus rose from the dead? Could this be an imaginative, exaggerated version of him recovering from a small flesh wound? Probably not. Such stories cannot be the result of an enthusiastic stretching of the truth. 'Bias' simply does not work like that.

Furthermore, just because someone is passionate about a particular subject—and therefore in some sense biased—it is hardly a good reason to dismiss their views on that topic. For instance, I am passionate and, therefore, 'biased' about my son, Joshua. He is a fantastic soccer player, a good singer and an outstanding wrestler—for a four-year-old. If you were to read an account of my son's life written by me, you might expect me to cast him in a favourable light, but does that mean my account will be untrustworthy? Of course not. In fact, it is precisely my great love and bias towards Josh that are likely to make me bother recalling and retelling the sorts of detail about him that a dispassionate observer is likely to miss entirely. Think of your own feelings about your wife, husband, partner, friend, mother, or whoever. Do you think these emotions would rule out your ability to produce an accurate written account of your loved one?

The reports upon which Luke's biography is based, and Luke's own reproduction of these reports, are no doubt affected by a great enthusiasm for the subject, but this is hardly a reason for thinking that they are also infected with an irrational stretching of the truth.

PROPHECIES OF THE COMING KING/CHRIST

THE 'ANOINTING' CEREMONY OF KING DAVID

In about 1000 BC a young man called David, son of Jesse, (of 'David and Goliath' fame) was selected to be the first in a long line of dynastic kings to rule ancient Israel. The ceremony by which he was made king established the importance of 'anointing' for the future hope concerning the 'Anointed One', or the Christ.

*The LORD said to Samuel, "How long will you mourn for Saul, since I have rejected him as king over Israel? Fill your horn with oil and be on your way; I am sending you to Jesse of Bethlehem. I have chosen one of his sons to be king"... Samuel did what the LORD said. When he arrived at Bethlehem, the elders of the town trembled when they met him. They asked, "Do you come in peace?" Samuel replied, "Yes, in peace; I have come to sacrifice to the LORD. Consecrate yourselves and come to the sacrifice with me." Then he consecrated Jesse and his sons and invited them to the sacrifice. When they arrived, Samuel saw Eliab and thought, "Surely the **LORD's anointed** stands here before the LORD." But the LORD said to Samuel, "Do not consider his appearance or his height, for I have rejected him. The LORD does not look at the things man looks at. Man looks at the outward appearance, but the*

*LORD looks at the heart." Then Jesse called Abinadab and had him pass in front of Samuel. But Samuel said, "The LORD has not chosen this one either." Jesse then had Shammah pass by, but Samuel said, "Nor has the LORD chosen this one." Jesse had seven of his sons pass before Samuel, but Samuel said to him, "The LORD has not chosen these." So he asked Jesse, "Are these all the sons you have?" "There is still the youngest," Jesse answered, "but he is tending the sheep." Samuel said, "Send for him; we will not sit down until he arrives." So he sent and had him brought in. He was ruddy, with a fine appearance and handsome features. Then the LORD said, "Rise and **anoint him**; he is the one." So Samuel took the horn of oil and **anointed him** in the presence of his brothers, and from that day on the Spirit of the LORD came upon David in power. (1 Samuel 16:1-13)*

Each king of Israel from this time on was known as an 'anointed one' (a messiah or christ), but they very rarely lived up to the role of speaking and acting on God's behalf. As the kingship declined, the prophets predicted the arrival of a descendant of King David who **would** speak and act on behalf of the Almighty and rule the nations for ever. On the basis of these prophecies, by the time we get to 200 BC much of the historical Jewish literature is crying out for THE ANOINTED ONE. Below is a brief outline of some of the elements of these promises.

THE PROMISE OF AN ETERNAL KING

Despite the length and greatness of King David's reign, the prophet Nathan promised David on God's behalf that one of his descendents would become even greater. According to the prophecy, this heir would rule for all of history.

*That night the word of the LORD came to Nathan, saying:
"Go and tell my servant David, 'This is what the LORD
says: "…When your days are over and you rest with your
fathers, I will raise up your offspring to succeed you, who will
come from your own body, and I will establish his
kingdom… I will establish the throne of his kingdom forever.
I will be his father, and he will be my son… Your house and
your kingdom will endure forever before me; your throne will
be established forever.' " Nathan reported to David all the
words of this entire revelation. (2 Samuel 7:4-17)*

In a matter of generations after king David, Israel and its
kings sank into religious, political and military turmoil. To
cut a long story short, by 587 BC the Jewish people had been
reduced to prisoners in their own land, and a great many of
them had been deported to surrounding nations. Foreign
armies had virtually destroyed them. The old promise of a
descendant of King David who would rule forever seemed
like a dim and ridiculous hope.

There were some, however, during the final years of Israel's
royal history, who did remember the promise Nathan relayed
to King David. These people were the 'prophets' and they
preached and wrote enthusiastically, during a time of great
pessimism, about God's intention one day to send that leader
of their dreams. Their writings, contained now in the Old
Testament part of the Bible, provide the clearest predictions
about the 'Anointed One', the descendent of David who
would reign eternally.

Here are four of the most significant prophecies concerning the eternal king, all of which were written hundreds
of years before the birth of Jesus.

EZEKIEL 37:22-25 (AROUND 600 BC).

"There will be one king over all of them and they will never again be two nations or be divided into two kingdoms. They will no longer defile themselves with their idols and vile images or with any of their offenses, for I will save them from all their sinful backsliding, and I will cleanse them. They will be my people, and I will be their God. "My servant David will be king over them, and they will all have one shepherd. They will follow my laws and be careful to keep my decrees. They will live in the land I gave to my servant Jacob, the land where your fathers lived. They and their children and their children's children will live there forever, and David my servant will be their prince forever.

Calling the future king "David" is a deliberate reflection on the promise quoted earlier that one of King David's son's will arise. Like that original promise, this prophecy also insists the king will rule forever. It is difficult to know how the Jews of this period would have understood this promise, since they, like us, knew that people do not live forever.

The Gospels of Luke and Matthew both begin with Jesus' genealogical records, establishing him as a direct descendent of King David, and they both end (as do all the Biographies) with the account of Jesus' resurrection. It is his resurrection, according to Jesus himself, that ensures his status as the king who rules forever.

The other interesting thing about this prophecy is that the arrival of the king will mark a time of forgiveness for past wrongs. As the story of Jesus unfolds, precisely this theme is highlighted again and again.

MICAH 5:2 (AROUND 740 BC)

A brief, though important, prophecy concerns the where-abouts of the coming ruler. In his prediction about what God would do for his people, Micah writes:

"But you, Bethlehem Ephrathah, though you are small among the clans of Judah, out of you will come for me one who will be ruler over Israel, whose origins are from of old, from ancient times."

Bethlehem is a small town in the South of Palestine, 10 km from the city of Jerusalem. Though small and apparently insignificant, it did have at least one claim to fame. It was the birth place and family home town of the great King David 300 years before. According to this prophecy, it would have an even greater claim to fame in the future. It would be the place from which the "ruler over Israel" (in other words, the promised anointed king) would come. Jesus, as we know from Luke (and elsewhere), was in fact born in the city of David, Bethlehem.

ISAIAH 9:1-7 (AROUND 740 BC)

Nevertheless, there will be no more gloom for those who were in distress. In the past he humbled the land of Zebulun and the land of Naphtali, but in the future he will honor Galilee of the Gentiles, by the way of the sea, along the Jordan—The people walking in darkness have seen a great light; on those living in the land of the shadow of death a light has dawned. You have enlarged the nation and increased their joy; they rejoice before you as people rejoice at the harvest, as men rejoice when dividing the plunder... For to us a child is born, to us a son is given, and the government will be on his shoulders. And he will be called Wonderful Counselor, Mighty God, Everlasting Father, Prince of Peace. Of the increase of his government and peace there will be no end. He will reign on David's throne and over his kingdom, establishing and upholding it with justice and righteousness from that time on and forever. The zeal of the LORD Almighty will accomplish this.

Here God promises that the Northern region of Palestine, Galilee, which was first to be decimated and overrun by 'Gentiles' (700 BC), will become the very district from which a great 'light' will appear. This will be the cause of great 'rejoicing' since the light turns out to be none other than the promised descendent of King David who would emerge from Galilee and rule forever.

On the face of it, this appears to contradict the prophecy of Micah that the promised 'ruler' would come from Bethlehem in the South of the country. For years, anyone who put these two texts side by side must have wondered how the anointed descendent of King David could come from both the Southern town of Bethlehem and the Northern district of Galilee, over a hundred kilometres away.

Though Jesus was born in the South of Palestine (in Bethlehem), this was only because of an unexpected Imperial requirement in that precise year that all Jews return to the town of their ancestors so that a documented census could take place throughout the land. Jesus' real home town—where he spent his entire childhood, right up to the time of his inaugural sermon—was, in fact, Nazareth, a town in the Northern district of Galilee. When the 'light' of Jesus' ministry appeared to the public eye, it was out of Galilee that it first shone.

ISAIAH 11:1-10 (AROUND 740 BC)

In this prophecy, the coming king is described as a 'shoot' from the 'stump of Jesse'. Jesse was King David's father. When Isaiah wrote these words, this family dynasty was already in tatters and on the verge of destruction, which is why it is described as a 'stump' instead of a whole tree. Nevertheless, the prophecy is clear: from this family line a 'branch' will grow.

> *A shoot will come up from the stump of Jesse; from his roots a Branch will bear fruit. The Spirit of the LORD will rest on him— the Spirit of wisdom and of understanding, the Spirit of counsel and of power, the Spirit of knowledge and of the fear of the LORD—and he will delight in the fear of the LORD. He will not judge by what he sees with his eyes, or decide by what he hears with his ears; but with righteousness he will judge the needy, with justice he will give decisions for the poor of the earth. He will strike the earth with the rod of his mouth; with the breath of his lips he will slay the wicked… In that day the Root of Jesse will stand as a banner for the peoples; the nations will rally to him, and his place of rest will be glorious.*

There are several important aspects of this prophecy. First, this descendant of David is described as ruling with his 'mouth', that is, by the mere force of his words. This must have sounded unusual to its first hearers since they must certainly have felt that what they needed was not a 'talker' but a 'warrior'. Jesus worked hard at dispelling the view that his was going to be a reign of warfare. Instead, he was indeed a great teacher. By his words he ruled.

Furthermore, it is odd that not only Israel but also all the nations would rally to this coming king. This idea was quite contrary to the political mood of both Isaiah's time and Jesus' time. The 'nations' were regarded as the enemies of God and Israel. Nevertheless, the prophecy is adamant that "the Root of Jesse will stand as a banner for the peoples; the nations will rally to him". In other words, this was a king for the world not just the Jews. This ends up being one of the very striking features of Jesus' ministry. He had an unusual openness to non-Jews whenever he met them. And in his final words to his colleagues he insisted that the news of his reign as the Christ must be "announced to all nations, beginning from Jerusalem" (Luke 24:47).

ISAIAH 52:13–53:12 (AROUND 700 BC)

The final and most striking prophecy I will quote (although there are many others) comes again from the prophet Isaiah. Here Isaiah speaks of the appearance of a mysterious figure known as the 'Servant'. There are no names or dates provided, but he is described as a "tender shoot" who "grew up out of the dry ground". This is clearly a reference back to the prophecy just quoted about the 'shoot' that grew up out of the 'stump of Jesse'. In other words, both prophecies are a reference to the promised descendant of King David. But there is an extraordinary difference between this and all the other prophecies about the future anointed king. Whereas most of the prophecies describe this figure as a powerful and majestic monarch, someone who rules the nations forever merely by the words of his mouth, the promise of Isaiah 52–53 describes him as a suffering and dying 'servant'. The passage is long but it is remarkable when you keep in mind that we know this was written hundreds of years before the birth of Jesus of Nazareth.

See, my servant will act wisely; he will be raised and lifted up and highly exalted. Just as there were many who were appalled at him—his appearance was so disfigured beyond that of any man and his form marred beyond human likeness—so will he sprinkle many nations, and kings will shut their mouths because of him. For what they were not told, they will see, and what they have not heard, they will understand. Who has believed our message and to whom has the arm of the LORD been revealed? He grew up before him like a tender shoot, and like a root out of dry ground. He had no beauty or majesty to attract us to him, nothing in his appearance that we should desire him. He was despised and rejected by men, a man of sorrows, and familiar with suffering. Like one from whom men hide their faces he was despised, and we esteemed him not. Surely he took up our infirmities and carried our sorrows, yet we considered him stricken by God, smitten by him, and afflicted. But he was pierced for our transgressions, he was crushed for our iniquities; the punishment that brought us peace was upon him, and by his wounds we are healed. We all, like sheep, have gone astray, each of us has turned to his own way; and the LORD has laid on him the iniquity of us all. He was oppressed and afflicted, yet he did not open his mouth; he was led like a lamb to the slaughter, and as a sheep before her shearers is silent, so he did not open his mouth. By oppression and judgment he was taken away. And who can speak of his descendants? For he was cut off from the land of the living; for the transgression of my people he was stricken. He was assigned a grave with the wicked, and with the rich in his death, though he had done no violence, nor was any deceit in his mouth. Yet it was the LORD's will to crush him and cause him to suffer, and though the LORD makes his life a guilt offering, he will see his offspring and prolong his days, and the will of the LORD will prosper in his hand. After the suffering of his soul, he will see the light of life and be satisfied; by his knowledge my righteous servant will justify many, and he will bear their iniquities. Therefore I will give him a portion among the great, and he will divide the spoils with the strong, because he poured out his life unto death, and was numbered with the transgressors. For he bore the sin of many, and made intercession for the transgressors.

I've known about this prophecy for over a decade but I am still amazed by its message. This 'Servant' of God would not attain 'majesty' but instead be 'pierced' and 'wounded'. He would die a horrible death—"cut off from the land of the living"—for the sake of others. He would be punished for the 'sins' of others so they could be forgiven. Eventually, however, this Servant would again "prolong his days" and "see the light of life". In other words, he would be raised from death. This story of tragedy to triumph would, according to the introduction to the prophecy, touch the whole world; he would "sprinkle many nations".

For a text composed more than half a millennium earlier, this is not a bad summary of the story of Jesus Christ, the promised descendant of David whose life, death and resurrection have, indeed, 'sprinkled' many nations.

THE RESURRECTION OF CHRIST

In the past, people have tried to rule out the entire discussion about 'resurrection' as absurd. They have said, "In our consistent human experience, dead people just do not come back to life. Therefore, Jesus could not have been raised from the dead either." That is, because we have never seen a resurrection, we rule it out as a possibility. This 'logic' was most forcefully stated by the renowned 18th century English philosopher, David Hume. He argued that our solid 'background evidence' about the reliability of the laws of nature should override all 'foreground claims' about the abrogation of those laws, or 'miracles'. At first, this seems reasonable. The fact that I've never seen a pink and polka dot coloured elephant, combined with the fact that I know they consistently come in gray, would make me extremely sceptical if anyone claimed to have seen such a creature.

However, there are a number of holes in Hume's argument, as many modern philosophers have been keen to point out.[†]

---

† For instance, see the article by the Oxford University Professor of Philosophy, Richard Swinburne. R. Swinburne. "Evidence for the Resurrection", in *The Resurrection: An Interdisciplinary Symposium on the Resurrection of Jesus.* Oxford: Oxford University Press, 1998, pp.191-212.

Human observation, whether personal or scientific, does not establish in full the fixity of natural laws. For example, if you lived in England two centuries ago, you would have been brought up to believe that all swans were white. You would have dismissed the rumours about black swans (coming from Southern Hemisphere countries like Australia and South Africa) as hoaxes or a case of mistaken identity. But the fact of the matter is that black swans did exist, even though the English had never seen them. Limited observation can only tell you what to predict, not what actually is. So, an 18th century Englishman could not rightly say, "I have never seen a black swan, therefore they do not exist". He could only say, "The evidence available to me leads me to expect that black swans do not exist".

Thus, the critical issue is **evidence**. There is no disputing that in our experience resurrections from the dead do not happen. But this alone cannot rule out a resurrection on a particular occasion. The question must be asked: Is the 'foreground evidence' about Jesus' resurrection sufficient to challenge, or at least create an exception to, the 'background evidence' concerning the normal function (or rather non-function) of a dead body? In other words, is evidence for Jesus rising from the dead strong enough to contradict our expectation that such things do not happen?

I think there are four pieces of evidence that suggest Jesus was raised from the dead. I'll present each of them and then raise some arguments against them. You can be the judge of whether or not the evidence is strong.

EVIDENCE ONE: *Jesus' tomb was corpse-less*
One of the most compelling arguments for Jesus' resurrection is the fact that it is almost beyond doubt that Jesus' tomb was

THE RESURRECTION OF CHRIST

empty a short time after his execution.

There are three things that put the empty tomb beyond reasonable doubt.

REASON ONE: *Jesus' resurrection was proclaimed in Jerusalem just weeks after the crucifixion.*
This is very important. If Jesus' tomb was not empty, such preaching could not have taken place. The tomb was owned by a prominent politician of the time named Joseph of Arimathea and so could easily be found by anyone who wanted to know. How on earth would the apostles have gotten away with telling people in Jerusalem (where Jesus was buried) that they had seen Jesus alive and well, without a body being produced to contradict them? Let me put it like this. Down at Balmoral Beach in Mosman, Sydney (near where I live), there is a statue of a dog named 'Billy'. He was a well-known canine in the area years ago. Suppose next week I claim to have seen the statue of Billy the wonder dog come to life and run away. Now, I might just get away with that claim in Perth, New Zealand or Wales (no offence intended), where no-one could check up on me. But I couldn't get away with it in Mosman itself. Mosman residents could too easily take a drive down to the beach and prove me a liar. The fact is, the first public claim of Jesus' resurrection occurred less than five kilometres from his burial site. This is a strong reason for believing that the tomb was, in fact, empty.

REASON TWO: *Jesus' tomb did not become a holy site in the years immediately after his death.*
This doesn't sound very interesting on its own, I know. But what is odd, is that during the time of Jesus there were at least 50 tombs of great Jewish religious leaders in Palestine, and all

of these sites were considered to be holy sites. A fair bit of religious activity took place at them. So, the question needs to be asked: If Jesus' corpse remained in the tomb, why was this custom not followed?

REASON THREE: *The Jewish leaders did not contest the empty tomb.*

In Matthew's biography, it is clear that the popular argument against Jesus' resurrection in the years following the claim did not revolve around whether the tomb was empty but **how** it became empty. It was assumed, even by those who violently opposed the disciples' claim, that the tomb of Jesus was vacant and had been from a couple of days after his execution. There's even an ancient document a hundred years after Matthew's Gospel that records a debate between a Jewish intellectual named Trypho and a Christian leader named Justin. In the document, it is clear the Jews of that time still did not argue against the tomb being empty. They simply raised suspicion about how it came to be empty!

So the obvious question is, "How did the tomb come to be empty?" Here are a few possible explanations.

COUNTER-ARGUMENT ONE: *Perhaps Jesus didn't die on the cross, but simply fell unconscious, was buried, and later got better in the tomb.*

According to this explanation, Jesus unwrapped his own burial clothes, rolled away the boulder that blocked the entrance, walked for two or three kilometres, showed himself to his friends and was somehow able to convince them that God had powerfully raised him to a new life. All I can say to this explanation is that it used to be argued. Modern scholars are now embarrassed that this argument was ever raised. The more we've learnt about Roman execution practices in the period, the more implausible it looks that Jesus 'got better' in the tomb, let alone convinced his friends that he was powerfully alive and well.

COUNTER-ARGUMENT TWO: *Perhaps they went to the wrong tomb on Sunday morning.*
Jesus' tomb was visited by some women who were his followers. They were the ones who discovered the tomb was empty. Some people have suggested they visited the wrong tomb.

This explanation surmises that the tomb Mary and the other women visited looked like the one Jesus had been placed in, but in actual fact was another one that happened to be unused. Thus, the whole of Christianity is based on a couple of people losing their way in the night. This explanation faces the very serious problem that sooner or later someone would have checked again. Remember, the tomb where Jesus was buried was owned by one of the prominent politicians of the time. It could easily have been accessed and the women's mistake would have been revealed.

COUNTER-ARGUMENT THREE: *Perhaps the disciples stole the body.*
This is the oldest explanation of the empty tomb (actually the second oldest behind the claim that he was, in fact, raised!). It's the one Jewish people have used ever since the 1st century. For me, though, it is also the hardest to accept. Think of it this way. Suppose I stand up in church next week and claim to have seen the statue of 'Billy' the wonder dog come to life and run away. After a thorough search of Balmoral Beach, it

is discovered that the statue is missing. Within weeks I'm a national celebrity. A radio talk-show host invites me onto his show and praises me for having seen a modern miracle. TV current affairs reporters ring me offering a million dollar contract for the exclusive rights to a step-by-step re-enactment of the miracle. Media moguls want to publish my story, and Oxford University invites me for a lecture tour. What would you conclude? I'm sure some of you would be thinking, "I bet he stole the statue for his own personal gain". That's what I would conclude too.

But suppose things went the other way, and I had nothing to gain by my lie. The talk-show host grills me for being a scam artist. The reporters expose me as a fraud. My family disowns me. The media mogul prints an article about the stupidity of my belief. I am eventually taken to court and tried for 'public deception', and then taken to prison until I admit to the truth. If I had stolen the statue, how long do you think it would take before I confessed to my deception? Not long I think.

The same problem applies to Jesus' resurrection. If the disciples had become rich and famous for their claims about Jesus, it would be easier to conclude that they stole the body from the tomb and made up this incredible resurrection story. But the opposite is true. They were considered 'heretics' and 'traitors' by many of their fellow Jews. They were taken to court and thrown in prison. And many of them were, in fact, executed (for the names, dates and methods of execution for some of these eyewitness, see p.207 in 'Extra Information I'). Why, if they knew they had merely taken the body from the tomb, did they die for the claim that Jesus was raised from the tomb? It is true that plenty of people throughout history have suffered and died for beliefs they did not know were wrong, but who on earth would willingly die for something they knew was a lie? It is an extremely difficult historical and psychological question to answer without a resurrection.

In my opinion, none of these attempts to explain away the empty tomb succeeds. This brings me back to my first piece of evidence. It seems beyond reasonable doubt that the tomb of Jesus was actually corpse-less on Easter Sunday morning, and no attempt to explain it away satisfies the facts.

Let me offer a few more pieces of evidence for the resurrection of Jesus.

EVIDENCE TWO: *Women were the first witnesses to the resurrection.*

One of the interesting features of the biographies of Jesus is that they all claim that women were the first people to witness the event. This may not sound like a very big deal to modern readers, but in 1st century Palestine it was a very significant point. A woman's testimony was considered untrustworthy by 1st century Jewish leaders, so much so that they were not allowed to give evidence in a court of law. So, for instance, first century Jewish historian Josephus writes about certain requirements in court:

> *But let not a single witness be credited, but three, or two at the least, and those such whose testimony is confirmed by their good lives.* **But let not the testimony of women be admitted, on account of the frivolity and boldness of their sex.** *Nor let servants be admitted to give testimony, on account of the ignobility of their soul.* (Josephus The Antiquities of the Jews, Book 4, chapter 8.)

I know this sounds incredibly unjust, but I raise this only to illustrate the legal situation of the time (incidentally, the fact that women were the first to witness the resurrection shows that God had no problem with their testimony).

So, if you were making up a story about a resurrection and you wanted your fellow 1st century Jews to believe it, why would you include women as the initial witnesses, unless of course it just happened to be embarrassingly true? All four biographies agree that women were the first to witness Jesus' resurrection.

EVIDENCE THREE: *Similarities and dissimilarities in the accounts.*

Like police assessing the evidence of witnesses, historians look not only for general agreement between various accounts of a particular event (convergence) but also for small individual variations (divergence). The slight divergence tells you the witnesses haven't simply copied each other's stories.

The Gospels live up to this convergence/divergence test. On the one hand, the different accounts agree in profound ways. For example, they agree on the day it occurred and that it was morning when it happened. They agree that women were the first to realise the resurrection had taken place. And they agree that there was confusion and doubt among the apostles when they first heard that Jesus was raised. However, someone could look at all this 'agreement' and argue that the biographers just got together and made sure they all said the same thing. But the reality is there are also significant differences between the biographies. And some of these differences are very difficult (though not impossible) to reconcile with each other. For example, Mark's biography says that just after daylight on Sunday morning, three women first went to the tomb. John's biography, however, mentions only one woman, and she apparently visited while it was still dark.

My point is, if all the accounts were full of contradictions you could conclude they were not trustworthy. But if they were identical, word for word, you could conclude there was a planned scam or cover-up. But neither looks likely. The different biographies display both profound agreement and significant variation.

EVIDENCE FOUR: *Transformation of the disciples.*
A fourth piece of evidence for the resurrection is the amazing transformation of Jesus' disciples after Easter Sunday. How did a small group of uneducated Jewish people become so adamant about their leader's resurrection that they confidently claimed, proclaimed, debated, stood trial, suffered and, in some cases, died, for that claim? And, how on earth did devout 1st century Jews (who naturally avoided other races and nations), begin the largest, most international and multicultural religion in the world?

Let me give you an individual example of the transformation that took place in one of Jesus' followers. In the biographies, it is clear that Jesus' own brothers did not believe in him. In fact, according to Mark's biography, early on, they thought their famous brother was insane. However, in the Bible book called 'Acts', which describes the first years of the church after Jesus' resurrection, one of Jesus' brothers, James, has become a key leader of the early church. And, as you may remember from earlier in the book, the Jewish historian in this period, Josephus, even records something about James we don't hear about in the Bible—that he was eventually executed for his belief in his older brother. How did this happen? What stands between the unbelief of James recorded in the biographies and his willingness to be executed for believing in the risen Jesus? What caused such a transformation if it was not that he had seen his brother raised from death? This is only one example. Several, if not most, of the first apostles were eventually executed for their belief in the risen Jesus. What caused such fearless devotion?

Over the years, there have been a number of attempts to explain away this transformation. Here are a few of them.

COUNTER-ARGUMENT ONE: *Perhaps Jesus' disciples were inclined toward belief in resurrection.*
One explanation has suggested that Jesus' followers were already theologically biased toward believing in resurrections, and so it would not have taken very much for them to think that their beloved teacher was alive.

The first version of this explanation insists they were influenced by the *common Jewish belief that the dead can be raised.* But this is plainly wrong. There were two schools of thought in Jewish society at this time and neither believed in the type of resurrection the apostles claimed about Jesus. Sadducees (the ruling class of Israel) denied any possibility of resurrection. As far as they were concerned, when you're dead, you're dead. The Pharisees (a large sect of strict Jews) on the other hand did believe in resurrection from the dead. However, they believed there was one resurrection only, and that this event occurred for all of humanity at the end of history—the day of judgement. As far as we know, the claim of a solo resurrection in history was not, for Jews of this time, part of their world-view.

So, when the disciples came out saying they had seen Jesus

raised from the dead, they were not showing their Jewish influences at all. They were, in fact, defying those influences. Their claim was as strange and unique in their day as it is in ours. As Dr. A. E. McGrath of Oxford University, says

The history of Israel is littered with the corpses of pious Jewish martyrs, none of whom were ever thought of as having been raised from the dead in such a manner. (A.E. McGrath, Bridge-building, IVP, Leicester, 1992, p. 162)

Others attribute the disciples 'bias' toward belief in resurrection to *Greek myths about dying and rising gods.* It is true there are stories in Greek mythology which centre around gods who die and rise again, but these are presented *as* myths. They are written in the literary style of mythology, and have no historical placement or appeal to eyewitnesses. To quote McGrath again:

… there are no known instances of this myth being applied to any specific historical figure in pagan literature… the New Testament documents with some care give the place and the date of both the death and the resurrection of Jesus, as well as identifying the witnesses to both.(p.162-163)

In addition to this, according to the Greek philosophical view of the universe at this time, a resurrection involving a *real physical body* that could be touched, and that could eat, was absurd. But this is exactly what the apostles claimed. In fact, their claim was occasionally rejected by Greeks precisely because of this contradiction between Greek thought and the disciples' claim. Furthermore, it must be remembered that all of Jesus' disciples were Palestinian Jews. To them, Greek religious myths were blasphemous. To suggest that their central message came from such Greek myths is unlikely in the extreme, and very few historians today pursue this line of argument.

There are no reasons for thinking the disciples were favourably disposed or biased toward belief in Jesus' resurrection. If anything, their influences ran against such a claim, and yet they still made it.

COUNTER-ARGUMENT TWO: *Perhaps the disciples simply saw a 'vision'.*

Some people have suggested that what the apostles saw was not the raised body of Jesus, but some religious vision, like the kind spoken of in many religions. The basic problem with this explanation is that the Bible is full of 'visions' and is happy to name them as such. There is no question that the eyewitnesses (and biographers) of Jesus' resurrection knew the difference between a vision and a real event. However, nowhere do they speak of the resurrection as a vision. People who suggest the resurrection was simply a religious vision are left with a dilemma: why did people who were well acquainted with visions claim that the resurrection was a real physical event?

COUNTER-ARGUMENT THREE: *Perhaps the disciples hallucinated.*

Another explanation of the disciples' transformation suggests that after their terrible weekend—seeing their master executed, not sleeping or eating—the disciples may well have experienced hallucinations of Jesus which they thought were real. The problem with this explanation is that, to sane people, even hallucinations are clearly identifiable as such after the event. Secondly, you have the problem of explaining how over 500 people in many settings could have had the same hallucination over a forty day period.

THE RESURRECTION OF CHRIST

This transformation of the disciples is so difficult to explain that a leading ancient historian from Germany, Dr Pinchas Lapide, has admitted that Jesus' resurrection must have occurred. This is not so amazing by itself—many modern scholars believe Jesus rose from the dead. What is amazing is that Lapide is a devout Jew who adamantly opposes the Christian belief that Jesus was the Christ. Here is what he concludes:

> *How was it possible that his disciples, who by no means excelled in intelligence, eloquence, or strength of faith, were able to begin their victorious march of conversion…? In a purely logical analysis, the resurrection of Jesus is 'the lesser of two evils' for all those who seek a rational explanation of the worldwide consequences of that Easter faith. Thus according to my opinion, the resurrection belongs to the category of the truly real… (The Resurrection of Jesus: a Jewish perspective. London: SPCK, 1984)*

CONCLUSION

More could be said on this topic. For example, another obvious line of argument that contributes to the believability of the resurrection is the very existence of God. Put simply, if there is a God, raising someone from the dead would hardly be a difficult thing to pull off. The fact that 80% of Australians believe in the existence of God means that, for at least 14 million of us, the resurrection of a person claiming to be God's agent on earth should not be dismissed simply because resurrections don't normally occur. If the historical evidence points decisively in the direction of Jesus really rising from the dead, then our belief in the existence of an all-powerful Creator, who can do things like raise the dead, gets us philosophically over the line, and right between the posts!

Of course, if you don't believe in the existence of God, this piece of philosophical argumentation is of no value for you. But you are still left with the very difficult task of explaining how, historically speaking, it looks as though a man who said he would rise from the dead, did.

Let me close by recounting an interesting debate that took place.

On May 2nd and 3rd 1985, the philosophy faculty of Liberty University, Virginia USA, hosted a professionally adjudicated debate between the renowned scholar and atheist, Prof. Antony Flew, and an internationally recognised expert in the origins of Christianity, historian, Dr Gary Habermas. The topic of the debate was "The Historicity of the Resurrection: Did Jesus Rise from the Dead?" It was attended by 3000 people, and the transcripts of the debate have since been published as a book.[†]

Two panels of judges were employed for the debate. One consisted of five professional debate judges who were asked to judge "the argumentation technique of the debaters". The second panel consisted of five academic philosophers who were instructed "to judge the content of the debate and render a winner". All ten judges serve on the faculties of leading American universities and represented a wide spectrum of views and persuasions.

The panel of professional adjudicators, judging argumentation, voted three to two in favour of Habermas. The panel of philosophers, judging content, cast four votes for Habermas

---

† G. Habermas and A. Flew, *Did Jesus Rise from the Dead: The Resurrection Debate.* San Fransisco: Harper and Row, 1987.

and the fifth deemed the debate a draw. Overall, then, the debate was won convincingly seven to two (with one draw), in favour of the affirmative, that Jesus was raised from the dead.

Of course, this does not prove the resurrection. I refer to this important debate merely to point out that belief in the resurrection of Jesus is far from ridiculous. Despite our quite reasonable expectation (based on the 'background evidence' of the reliability of the laws of nature) that dead people do not come back to life, there is good 'foreground evidence' leading intelligent people to believe that an exception to the norm has occurred in the case of Christ; that 36 hours after his execution he was raised to life.

BEYOND THIS BOOK

Over the years, I've known many, many people who, on hearing the news about Christ, have decided to pursue its implications. So I thought it might be wise to add some concluding remarks about how to go beyond this book and make the realities of Jesus' life part of your own life.

The first thing I'd suggest is to keep reading the New Testament. You've read and hopefully appreciated Luke's contribution to the Bible, but perhaps you could turn to one of the other Gospels now and read the news again from another perspective. I'd suggest the *Gospel of Mark*, written perhaps a decade or more before *Luke*. It's the shortest of the four biographies of Jesus, and will take you only an hour or so to finish.

Once you've completed *Mark*, if you want to read on, try something different. A great number of the New Testament books are actually letters from the first apostles to the new Christian communities living in the cities around the Mediterranean (such as Rome, Corinth and Ephesus). *Colossians* was written by the Apostle Paul to the Christians in the Western Turkish city of Colossae. In it, he reminds them that being a Christian is not about following philosophical and ritualistic rules. Instead, it is about trusting God's love for us expressed in the death and resurrection of Jesus, and then reflecting that love in the way we treat each other. The letter is only about five pages long and it is a great read.

You could also read the letter of *James*—again, only about five pages in length—written by Jesus' own brother, in the decade or so after the resurrection. In it, he reminds his readers that our faith in Jesus Christ has very practical implications for the way we are to think, speak and act toward others.

As you read any of these biblical books, ask yourself: "What are the key things the writer was trying to communicate to these ancient Christians and how do they apply to me now?" Incidentally, if you don't own a Bible, they are widely available through any major book store. I'd recommend the translation called the New International Version (NIV).

Secondly, I'd suggest that you tell someone else of your intention to respond to the news about Christ. I'm thinking particularly of someone who already believes in Christ and would be able to offer you some help and reassurance. This has the additional benefit of clarifying your own response to Christ—articulating your thoughts to someone else is often the best way to crystallise them. Perhaps you were given this book by a friend or relative. They'd probably love to hear your response. Alternatively, if you stumbled across this book by yourself and/or can't think of anyone who'd be interested in your reactions, why not think about looking in on a local church somewhere. Most churches are nowhere near as daunting as their architecture implies. Actually, very often you'll discover that the warm, practical, encouraging attitude of Jesus himself has, in fact, filtered down to his modern followers.

Another suggestion I'd like to make may sound strange at first, but it really can be very helpful. If you've now read the news about Christ and want to 'repent' (to use Jesus' own words) and find God's forgiveness, why not tell this to God himself. Several times in the *Gospel of Luke* Jesus insisted that God hears and answers people's prayers (see for instance the beginning of Chapter 18). Why not take Jesus at his word and offer a prayer to your Maker expressing your response to Christ's life. The following words are not magical—like an incantation or mantra—but they may help you articulate something of your intention to follow Jesus Christ. Read through the prayer first, then simply repeat them (out loud if you like) addressing God himself.

Lord,
Thank you for sending Jesus, your Christ, into the world. Thank you for both his words and actions on your behalf. Thank you especially that he died for me and was raised to life by you.

I admit that I have lived at a distance from you, not treating you with the honour and obedience that you deserve as my Creator. I realise that I have offended you. I am truly sorry for this sin. Please forgive me.

From this time on, help me to acknowledge you with reverence and trust. Teach me also to love other people in practical ways—just as Jesus taught.

[If you would like any further help—e.g. in obtaining a Bible or finding a church or answering some questions—please feel free to contact the publisher of this book. See the contact details opposite the table of contents. Another good source of information about Christianity is the website at www.christianity.net.au.]

ALSO BY JOHN DICKSON

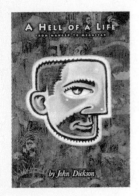

A Hell of a Life   *Hanging in There*   *A Sneaking Suspicion*

For more information about these books
and other Christian literature, call
Matthias Media or visit our website at:

www.matthiasmedia.com.au